PREFACE

The rough balances in the numbers of the two sexes that we have known in the past may not persist into the future. They may change in a number of ways. The natural process since time immemorial by which males have slightly but consistently outnumbered females at birth is now being altered by medical interventions, notably by the growing number of female abortions taking place in many developing countries with falling birth rates, particularly the world's two most populous countries, China and India. There is also the looming prospect that sex selection at birth will become commonplace in the more developed countries during the early decades of the twenty-first century and, like so many other phenomena, that it will be rapidly diffused and globalised, thus altering the ratio of male to female births. Does this mean that centuries of traditional son preference will begin to break down, and will it in some societies even be replaced by daughter preference as a result of the rapidly changing economic roles of women in many countries?

In any case, unless women are severely disadvantaged (as, for example, in some Asian cultures) they usually outlive men, and with nearly all populations experiencing increasing proportions of older people there are certain to be more older women than men. Unfortunately, large numbers of them will be widows who in many of the poorer countries often live in particularly difficult socio-economic circumstances of poverty and isolation. With these changing patterns of births, deaths and ageing of populations, will women begin to substantially outnumber men?

In addition to the so-called natural changes in population through births, deaths and ageing, the numerical balance of the two sexes in most parts of the world is being greatly transformed by a revolution in the speed, volume and extent of human mobility, particularly in the changing mobility of women, who for millennia have been much more linked to the hearth and home and have not migrated as far or as often as men. This was largely because they have been '*The Second Sex*' (1949), as Simone de Beauvoir entitled her seminal text that helped to give rise to contemporary feminism:

"One is not born, but rather becomes a woman. No biological, psychological, or economic fate determines the figure that the human female presents in society; it is civilisation as a whole that determines this creature".

Now, in most countries women are in a state of transition, not towards equality with men, but towards achieving their own identity. They are marrying later and having fewer babies, and they are also being educated more and assuming increasing roles in the labour force. One result is that they are moving about much more autonomously than ever before, especially over shorter distances and time spans, although the myriad of cultural differences to be found among the world's populations have had varied but important effects on their mobility. All this is taking place at a time when the world's total population has grown rapidly from 2.5 billion in 1950 to 6 billion in 1999, and is redistributing massively within the existing inhabited area through regional concentration in economic core areas, accelerated urbanisation and increasing localisation in large cities. Nearly half of the world's population are now living in a wide spectrum of towns and cities, with many mega-cities mushrooming in the Third World. Much of this concentration results from increased human mobility, especially female mobility. Is this greater female mobility, which is seen most of all in the more advanced countries where women have greater autonomy, likely to increase and be extended during the next century, and how will it affect the geographical distribution in the numerical balance of the sexes?

These are some of the many questions that will be addressed in this short book, which brings together many diverse strands, attempts to explain the basic issues on a world-wide basis, and looks at some of the prospects for the future. Examples are taken from numerous countries, perhaps more from those of Asia than of other continents, largely because that continent currently comprises about 59% of humanity living at differing levels of social and economic development. It thus provides many case studies of the problems associated with the changing balances of births, deaths and mobility of the two sexes. One certainty is that these balances have varied over time and space and will continue to do so. The profusion of contrasting cultures in the world, their variable persistence or modification, the social changes within them, and the ever-widening levels of economic development have all contributed to the considerable geographical and temporal diversity in the relative numbers of males and females. Of course, the diversity and changeability is most apparent among the smaller populations of localities, which vary much more than those of countries or continents, but they occur even at that compound level.

It is curious that few texts have attempted to review in any detail the variations in the numbers of males and females, despite growing public concern about the relative numbers of the two sexes in institutions, the workplace and elsewhere, and despite the rapidly expanding literature of gender studies, population studies and demography. Of course, many give summary statements concerning sex/gender compositions of populations, but few seek to explain why there are more males born than females, why older women are generally outnumbering older men or why there are differences in male and female mobility; in short, why the two sexes vary in numbers over time and space.

There is no simple explanation for this gap in the literature, although a number of reasons might be given. Perhaps the demographic data have been considered too imprecise for satisfactory research analyses. Perhaps it has been felt that the absolute differences between the numbers of males and females were insufficient in most populations to warrant such analysis. Perhaps the topic ranges too widely from the biological to the behavioural. Perhaps other matters were regarded as far too pressing and important. In the case of demography and population studies, there was undoubtedly a need to understand the dynamic processes of fertility, mortality and migration which have brought about such momentous population growth and redistribution during the second half of the twentieth century, in order that appropriate population policies might be formulated. Moreover, one might also point to the fact that until recently demography and population studies, like many other subjects, were largely male-dominated and that female issues were underplayed. Indeed, the urgent need within gender studies during the 1990s was to provide a less male-dominated approach and a better balance to our understanding of how gender has influenced social processes, as well as to encourage wholesale changes in social behaviour in order to improve the lot of girls and women world-wide.

In comparison with these dynamic processes which have been of great social concern during the second half of the twentieth century, the study of the numerical differences in the numbers of males and females in populations might have appeared less vital or significant. It might have seemed to be merely a matter of detail. Yet, as we shall see, the subject is gathering growing significance as scientific and technological advances accompanied by social and economic changes are affecting the lives of men and women, and altering the relative numbers of the births, deaths and mobility of the two sexes with the likelihood of many further dramatic changes in store. And some of these dramatic changes will take place within the world's largest populations, those of China and India.

The 1990s saw the emergence of a growing number of studies examining the influence of gender on human populations, especially on their mobility, and here credit can be given to many international and national institutions and organisations for organising conferences and seminars which helped to stimulate such developments. Certainly the author was able to benefit from many of these meetings. However, unlike many of my publications during the last two decades, done in collaboration with numerous colleagues from other countries mainly under the auspices of the International Geographical Union (IGU) Commission on Population Geography and the International Union for the Scientific Study of Population (IUSSP) Committee on Population and Environment, the writing of this book has been a more solitary effort, reflecting the space and opportunities of retirement and requiring little assistance apart from my computer, the internet and library sources. Nevertheless, the book would not have been completed without the support and forbearance of my dear wife, to whom my eternal thanks, or without the profound influence and affection of my three darling daughters and their families. I am also most grateful for help with the illustrations to David Hume, Steven Allan and Chris Orton of the Drawing Office and to Mike Cuthbertson of *r.cade* (Resource Centre for Access to

Data on Europe) in the Department of Geography of the University of Durham, and finally to Ann Marie Davenport and David Clark of Elsevier Science for seeing the book through to publication.

John I. Clarke
Durham

LIST OF FIGURES

LIST OF TABLES

CONTENTS

CHAPTER 1

SEX RATIOS AND GENDER

1.1 Biological Sex and Social Gender

Perhaps because people have always been looking for symmetry in what is essentially an asymmetrical world, we often think of males and females as a clear-cut division, a basic human dichotomy, that is also common to all other vertebrates and most of the natural world. This deep-seated division is reflected in all of our activities, so much so that society deems that there is a legal requirement for our biological sex to be registered as either male or female, with all sorts of ensuing social obligations and civic rights that affect our gender roles as males and females, the way that we perceive and choose ourselves to be.

The difference between our biological sex and our social gender was slow to be accepted in population studies, perhaps because their interaction is multifaceted and the distinction between them sometimes difficult to draw (Pollard and Hyatt, 1999). Although the concept of gender first appeared in the USA during the 1970s, the word 'gender' is not to be found in several demographic and geographic dictionaries published during the 1980s, and only became much more current during the 1990s with the mercurial rise in gender studies and the contemporaneous emergence of social demography. In this process, the work of the Committee on Gender and Population of the International Union for the Scientific Study of Population (IUSSP) has stimulated much scientific activity (e.g. Frederici *et al.*, 1993; Mason and Jensen, 1995), but in addition larger international organisations such as the ILO (see e.g. Oppong, 1987; Adepoju and Oppong, 1994), UNFPA and UNESCO have played very significant roles, as has the publicity engendered by major international conferences such as the Cairo conference on Population and Development in 1994 (Singh, 1998) and the Beijing conference on Women in 1995. Yet still too often gender roles are interpreted as female roles alone, especially by the public at large: too often gender means women.

1

Gender roles have profound effects on the demography of populations and are affected themselves by life-long processes of enculturation (Pollard and Hyatt, 1999: 2). "Gender is society's stereotype" and "cultural reinforcements of gender start in the cradle and end in the grave" (Potts and Short, 1999), with those cultural reinforcements varying substantially around the world. The major gender variations occur in the roles and norms of women, whose levels of literacy and education, age at first marriage and share of the workforce vary much more over time and space than those for men, greatly influencing their fertility, mortality and mobility and thus their numbers in any population.

After millennia of a male-dominated world, gender stereotypes are now under considerable attack and gender roles are being redefined. In many countries, especially some of the more advanced where women are taking over many of the roles formerly dominated by men, there is a gradual increase in the mixing of traditional male and female traits and characteristics, known as *androgyny*, in which for example women are encouraged to be more assertive and aggressive and men more integrative and caring. The division between the two sexes in their social and economic activities is becoming less sharp and more fuzzy. Some have even referred to this blurring of boundaries between the sexes, behaviourally rather than biologically, as the development of a 'third sex' or 'third gender'.

Certainly the biological sex of individuals has seemed to be much less ambiguous and more easily differentiated than their gender and most of their other social and cultural attributes, but recent researches have revealed that even the perceived biological dichotomy is rather less sharply defined than previously imagined. Doctors are occasionally posed with uncertainties concerning the certification of the sex of a child for the purposes of registration, made all the more difficult through knowing that it will be no easy task to persuade appropriate authorities of the need for a subsequent change in the registration.

Nevertheless, from this dichotomous biological standpoint of being either male or female, we have had a tendency to dichotomise many other phenomena, despite the fact that generally they fall much less neatly into two categories. We talk of rich and poor, black and white, ancient and modern, public and private, right and left, rural and urban, physical and human, East and West, North and South, developed and developing, white collar and blue collar ... the list could go on and on. These simple twofold classifications are less rigidly exclusive than the division of the sexes; they are dualisms rather than dichotomies which are meant to facilitate our understanding but are frequently responsible for over-simplifying broad spectra and immense complexities.

1.2   Sex and Gender Balances

Without the aid of statistics, we view populations from individual perspectives, and consequently most people probably assume that there are roughly equal numbers of males and females in the populations in which they live. People often say that 'women (or men) are half the world'. But is this really so? And if it is, will it remain so? There are not equal numbers of male and female births and deaths, nor do we move about in equal numbers, so it should not surprise us that the relative numbers of males and females vary quite substantially from place to place. In this volume we want to look at those variations, which are gaining considerable significance. With the aid of modern science and technology, not always of positive benefit, human populations are now able to influence as never before the relative numbers of births and deaths of the two sexes, thus altering their demographic balance. And because of the ever more rapid and global diffusion of scientific advances, this is true not just in the more advanced countries but in poor countries as well. In addition, there are also massive changes taking place in the mobility of men and women, at all levels from the immediate locality to the world as a whole, with considerable effects upon their relative numbers in localities, regions, countries and continents.

Certainly, if we look around us, there are rarely equal numbers of the two sexes. We often find ourselves in social groups which are more or less segregated or sorted by gender, especially at local level, as for example at school, work or play. In this book we focus primarily on the long-term variations in the balance of the two sexes, the sex ratios of resident populations caused by births, deaths and migrations, rather than on the shorter-lived variations and the social and economic determinants of the relative numbers of men and women at work or play. This latter phenomenon has come to be known in recent years as 'gender balance', which has gained increasing significance in human societies with the rising status and increasing autonomy of women and the diversification in their roles.

In particular, gender balance has become a target for many feminist groups working for female empowerment through better representation at all levels, socially, economically and politically, working on the basis that women's roles owe less to biology than to gender relationships largely determined by men. Their pressure has undoubtedly assisted increased feminine representation in innumerable companies, committees, departments, institutions, offices, organisations and political parties. Progress in gender balance in many of the more developed countries (MDCs) so far has been considerable but uneven. In contrast, it has been much less marked in those less developed countries (LDCs) where strong patriarchy persists and where unfortunately women still suffer to a greater or lesser extent from the prevalence of discrimination and subordination. However, the situation is ever-changing and hopefully we will see these deficiencies reduced much more as the twenty-first century proceeds, with greater diffusion and acceptance of gender balances.

Naturally, the terms 'sex balance' and 'gender balance' are not clearly distinguishable, because they are so closely interrelated. Although in simple terms the causes of gender balance are mainly social and those of sex balance are mainly

biological, it is extremely difficult to separate biological and social factors when
analysing these balances. It is also very difficult to distinguish between the biological and social influences upon births, deaths and mobility. Here in this book
we are interested in those diverse influences, especially in the impact of gender
roles on mortality and mobility. The latter is such an important element in human
differentiation and is so greatly affected by social and economic development that
currently population geographers at least are tending to use the term gender ratios
of mobility more than that of sex ratios.

Our main aim is to see how births, deaths and migrations affect the numbers
and balances of males and females in residential populations of all sizes, and how
they exhibit considerable and constantly changing diversity around the world.

1.3   Populations, Sub-populations, Area and Scale

We should bear in mind that for statistical enumeration populations are usually
defined by the administrative areas in which they live, rather than by their demographic distinctiveness. Because people have generally been counted by governments for political and administrative purposes, a population is usually defined as
the number of people living within a particular country or territorial division of a
country, rather than as a particular human grouping of genetic, ethnic or cultural
significance, in spite of the enormous influence of cultural factors upon demographic characteristics. In this way, population numbers have been regarded as
'fictive spaces', the spaces acquiring the attributes of the numbers. Yet the territories of countries and administrative districts differ immensely in size, shape and
geography, and their political boundaries have had diversely divisive effects upon
populations, some acting as real demographic divides (e.g. North and South
Korea) while others are crossed freely (e.g. Belgium and Luxembourg) and have
imperceptible effects upon the populations they separate. All this has greatly
affected the size, distribution, composition and dynamics of populations, impeding
rational comparisons between them (Clarke, 1973; 1976; 1997).

Thus, when we talk of the relative numbers of males and females in a population, we are generally referring to the population of a given area, usually a state or
a sub-division of a state, and should remember that apart from the world population as a whole, the populations and areas considered are hierarchical parts of
larger populations and areas and very much influenced by them. This is all the
more meaningful in an age when globalisation is having increasing influence upon
the most intimate aspects of life (e.g. family planning and family size; status of
women), and at the same time is constantly undermining the separateness of the
nation state, which was in the first place one of the main reasons for the collection
of population data and for the emergence of population studies as a form of
political arithmetic. The massive global movements of people, goods and ideas
and the ever-changing political map, including the creation of more and more

states and regional groupings, lead many to question the future of the state as we came to know it during the twentieth century (Blake, 1999). Although the existing 260 or so sovereign and dependent countries wish to retain their discrete identities, their populations are generally much less separate than they were before globalisation gathered pace, and they will become even less distinctive as their borders become less significant demographic boundaries.

In contrast to whole populations, male and female populations are not usually territorially exclusive. Rarely is the population of a territory wholly male or female. Male and female populations are particular types of *sub-populations*, specific elements of whole populations, just in the same way as are, for instance, aged, widowed, illiterate, employed, Welsh-speaking, foreign and Jewish populations. Sub-populations vary greatly in size over time and space, and on the whole are only territorially exclusive at a very local level, in special places such as an old people's home, a boys' school, an ethnic ghetto, an army barracks, a monastery or a convent. Male and female sub-populations tend to be only territorially separate in sex-segregated institutions, but over recent decades in many developed countries at least there has been a considerable reduction in institutional sex segregation, as schools, colleges, clubs, armed forces and workforces have become more mixed. Usually, the sexes are to a greater or lesser extent integrated, living and working together, with the ratio of the two sexes, the sex ratio, varying considerably from place to place.

We should also emphasise that, as in the case of so many other population phenomena, the balance of the sexes varies greatly with the scale of analysis. As far as we know, and nobody can be certain because precise statistics are not available, the aggregate numbers of males and females in the world as a whole appear to be not very dissimilar, but this balance may be illusory because, as we shall see, there is real concern about the millions of 'missing women' in certain parts of the world. Simply by aggregating national population data, it appears superficially as if there is a slight surplus of males, with the average sex ratio for the world population as a whole being about 101.5 males per 100 females in 1995 (United Nations, 1999). However, this cannot be regarded as an accurate figure, merely an approximation, because it is calculated from over two hundred national censuses taken at different times and with diverse levels of precision.

Coming down from the global population to look at smaller and smaller populations, we see increasing diversity in population structures including the relative numbers of males and females (Clarke, 1973; 1976), and this has been demonstrated using different sizes of grid square data (Clarke and Rhind, 1976). Naturally, the variations in sex ratios tend to be very much greater and more changeable at ward/parish levels than at larger sub-national and national levels. Local socio-economic conditions are influential, especially where certain economic activities such as mining have attracted single-sex labour forces and where educational, religious, military and penal establishments have meant that sex segregation has prevailed over integration.

1.4 Underlying Causes of Variations

Although focusing mainly on national populations, we shall look at the numerical balance of the sexes at various scales from the local to the global, and in particular at the three underlying reasons whose influences vary greatly over time and space and are not mutually exclusive:

- There is generally a preponderance of male births in populations, but numerically this has been the least important overall influence upon sex ratios in the past, because the surplus of male births in large populations is usually not more than a few per cent, there being of course much greater variability in the numbers of male and female births among small populations. However, there are signs are that preponderance of male births may well become a more important factor in the future.
- Sex-differential mortality, especially the preponderance of male deaths and the greater longevity of females, has been a less consistent but more numerically influential factor, especially among the ageing populations of today where older women are outnumbering men. At the global level, the influence of sex-differential mortality is the dominant influence upon sex ratios.
- Gender differences in mobility, especially migration, tend to vary greatly. Migration is very spasmodic and irregular over time and space, but it may have important local effects because the annual numbers of migrants to or from a particular locality are often larger than the numbers of either births or deaths. In general, the influence of migration on the relative numbers of males and females diminishes with increasing areal scale, because larger territories tend to incorporate more migrations within them, to the point where migration has, so far, had no effect upon the sex ratio of the global population.

The sex ratio of a population is not merely a consequence of the dynamic factors of fertility, mortality and migration; conversely, it has important demographic effects upon them and upon the incidence of marriage and/or cohabitation. Indeed, it has ramifications for the whole structure and nature of society. Consequently, it has been regarded as a basic aspect of demographic analysis, and the sex of an individual is an indispensable question in any census or registration enumeration.

We should also remind ourselves that we live in times of dramatic demographic change, when the spiralling world population growth of the second half of the twentieth century is beginning to succumb to some slowing down, both relatively and absolutely, brought about by a global diffusion of family limitation and fertility decline (Clarke, 1997). Nevertheless, it attained a total of six billion in 1999 (when India achieved a total of one billion), double the world total of 1960 and it was still increasing by about 78–80 million a year. Recent projections by the United Nations, World Bank, US Bureau of Census and the International Institute for Applied Systems Analysis all suggest that demographic transitions in nearly all countries will continue and be completed during the twenty-first century. The expected world population total in the middle of that century will be several billion lower than previously forecast, although growth will remain rapid in Africa, South and West Asia and Latin America and the total at the end of the century may well be about 10 billion (Bongaarts and Bulatao, 1999).

In addition, although less strikingly, there is a distinct possibility of considerable changes in the ratio of males to females. The most notable of these changes arises primarily from the inevitable effect of the improved life expectancy and widespread ageing of populations on the preponderance of older women, but also from the unfortunately growing incidence of sex predetermination through sex-selective abortion and from the realistic long-term prospect of the sex selection of babies. In addition, there is every reason to expect a continuation in the remarkable increase in the employment and geographical mobility of women, greatly influencing local gender balances. We shall examine all of these factors, as well as other phenomena, in succeeding chapters.

1.5 Measures of Sex Ratios

We have already referred to sex ratios, and we should now define what we mean by them quantitatively. Although the sex ratios of populations are most commonly expressed as the number of males per 100 females, unfortunately there is no single measure that is universally used (Shryock *et al.*, 1973). Three distinct measures are commonly found in the literature about populations, where Pm = the male population, Pf = the female population and Pt = the total population:

- *Masculinity proportion, or percentage males:* $\dfrac{Pm}{Pt} \times 100$

  This measure varies around 50%, and is used in a number of countries, including former republics of the USSR.

- *Masculinity ratio, or sex ratio:* $\dfrac{Pm}{Pf} \times 100$ (i.e. males per 100 females)

  Obviously, anything over 100 means an excess of males. This measure, used in the United States and by the United Nations organisations, is the most common index and the one used in this book.

- *Excess (or deficit) of males as a percentage of the total population:*

  $$\frac{Pm - Pf}{Pt} \times 100$$

  where 0 = a balance of the numbers in each sex, and positive values mean an excess of males.

The three measures can be easily converted as follows:

- Masculinity proportion $= \dfrac{\text{sex ratio}}{1 + \text{sex ratio}} \times 100$

- Sex ratio $= \dfrac{\text{masculinity prop.}}{1 - \text{masculinity prop.}} \times 100$

- Percentage excess males $= [\text{masculinity prop.} - (1 - \text{masculinity prop.}) \times 100]$

All the three measures have been sometimes expressed otherwise, as femininity proportions and ratios and as females as a percentage of the total population. Thus, in India, where for a variety of reasons there appears to be a shortage of females, the census defines sex ratios as the number of females per 1000 males. Some East European countries, where shortages of males occur, express sex ratios as the number of females per 100 males, as does New Zealand, and in recent years so have some feminist authors writing about gender issues and the status of women (e.g. Neft and Levine, 1997). To avoid confusion, we shall stick largely to the most common ratio as used by the United Nations, i.e. the number of males per 100 females, although occasionally the local practice is cited, especially in relation to the important case studies from India.

It should also be noted that because sex ratios are greatly influenced by age structures, their statistical comparability is diminished. Consequently, cartographers mapping sex ratios of large and diverse populations, as for example in Europe, have sometimes for purposes of comparability used *standardised masculinity ratios*, whereby the sex ratios by age of different regions are applied to the age structure of the whole country, the numbers of expected males and females are summed and standardised ratios created (e.g. Decroly and Vanlaer, 1991).

As sex ratios also vary considerably from one population sub-group to another, the sex ratio of the total population of a country, province or district may be regarded as a weighted average of the diverse sex ratios of other component sub-populations, such as age groups, ethnic groups and urban and rural populations. The component rates are weighted in proportion to the female proportion of each sub-population.

As far as demographic analysis is concerned, the most important variation in sub-group sex ratios is that of age groups. Accordingly, *age-specific sex ratios* are often calculated to identify the relative proportions of males and females in different cohorts and at different age groups within the life cycle. In general, sex ratios decline with age. Males tend to be relatively more numerous among younger populations and populations with high birth rates than among older populations and populations with low birth rates, but, as always, there are notable exceptions which will be highlighted in later chapters.

The *sex ratio score* is a method to check on the accuracy of age group data, which are affected by factors such as the under-reporting of certain age groups and the over-reporting of persons aged 5, 10, 15, 20, etc. It is based on the assumption that the numbers and sex ratio of each age group should change smoothly with increasing age, and is calculated by measuring the differences from a steady trend, irrespective of whether they are plus or minus, and by making no allowance for the expected decline of sex ratios with age. The mean difference between the sex ratios of all the pairs of successive age groups is the sex ratio score, and a score of 1.5 is suggested (United Nations, 1955) as the standard for evaluating any age distribution.

1.6   How Accurate are the Numbers?

Separate accurate data about the two sexes are important in our analysis of many other demographic data, in our understanding of many social, economic and political phenomena, for the planning of all manner of public and private facilities and amenities, and are therefore a vital if not always attainable feature of population censuses and surveys.

From the start, it has to be said that data on sex compositions of populations are not as accurate as once was assumed. Certainly, the data are easier to assemble than on most other population characteristics, but the statement by Shryock, Siegel and Associates (1973) in their masterly volume *The Methods and Materials of Demography* that "the definition and classification of sex present no statistical problems" is certainly questionable, and unless one is very sure of the validity of the data one should generally give little credence to sex ratios taken to several places of decimals. In many aspects of population study, only crude counts or rough estimates are available. We should recognise that there is always a danger of relying too readily on statistical data of populations, and certainly we should not overconcern ourselves with their digital precision.

Aggregate population data depend largely upon population censuses and surveys, which vary greatly in their periodicity, universality and reliability, being generally more regular, comprehensive and accurate in the wealthier MDCs than in the poorer LDCs. We should emphasise that the above widely used dualism of economic categories, MDCs and LDCs (also given a variety of other names such as North/South, rich/poor, developed/developing, advanced/ less advanced), is far from clear-cut. It is also increasingly unsatisfactory for use in population studies as there is now much less contrast in stages of demographic transition between the two groups of countries than there was in the middle of the twentieth century. Because the dualism remains in vogue and still has some utility, we use it from time to time in this book, but we must remember that the diverse demographies of countries range immensely in population size, density, distribution and dynamics and that economic development is only one factor in that diversity. Some LDCs have recently achieved in a few decades as much demographic transition from high to low birth and death rates as some MDCs had earlier achieved over a century, while others, especially some of the least developed countries (LLDCs), have made much less progress (Bongaarts and Bulatao, 1999). So there is more of a series of demographic spectra of populations than a dualism based upon level of development.

In addition, the accuracy of censuses is not merely dependent upon economic development, but also depends greatly on the degree of governmental organisation and administrative control over populations and territory. Some governments of LDCs (e.g. Afghanistan, Cambodia, Ethiopia) have had so little control over peripheral parts of their territories and populations that they have for long periods been incapable of holding a reliable comprehensive census, while other much more populous countries (e.g. China and India) are able to do so because of their closer network of administrative control. It follows that aggregating country population data to global, continental or MDC/LDC levels gives only indicative rather than reliable results.

Apart from censuses and surveys, the other main source of population data is the vital registration of births, marriages, deaths and the registration of population movements, but that is even more woefully deficient in many parts of the world, notably (but not exclusively) in some of the poorer countries of Sub-Saharan Africa and South Asia, and among ethnic minorities. For example, the United Nations Children's Fund (UNICEF) in its report *Progress of Nations 1998* estimated that as many as 40 million births a year went unregistered, about one-third of all births in the world! This staggeringly inadequate registration of births, which is particularly applicable to girls who in many poorer countries are regarded as the second sex, is most prevalent in those countries where babies are usually born outside of hospitals. Unless the lack of registration is rectified at a later date, it may well greatly affect their subsequent incorporation into society, including their access to health care services, education and employment as well as their reproductive behaviour (Jejeebhoy, 1995).

Whatever their level of accuracy, all population censuses and most other population counts ask a question about the sex of a person, although there are deficiencies in this respect in some types of migration data. Because of its importance to numerous aspects of society and economy, it is one of very few questions almost always asked. With only two suggested answers (male or female?), this basic question appears very simple in comparison with many other questions that have numerous possible responses, such as those concerning age of respondent, type of occupation, level of education, degree of literacy, languages spoken, nationality, ethnic origin, type of housing, or size and composition of household. One might therefore tend to assume that the data about sex are reasonably accurate. Unfortunately, accuracy is not nearly as reliable as expected. Yet despite the possibility of data inaccuracies, the sex ratios of countries are sometimes used to measure the quality of census data of age and sex, because they do not vary as much as many other demographic phenomena, and are independent of the absolute numbers of males and females.

1.7 Some Causes of Data Inaccuracies

Several factors lead to inaccuracies, some negligible, some much more significant. Although certainly a minor factor numerically, the dichotomy of the sexes
is not so clear as once was thought, biological differences being sometimes
blurred. The apparently simple choice of male or female for purposes of registration, which is so important legally, is not so simple for some individuals of
sexual indeterminacy. Recent studies of human chromosomes have revealed
many more cases of so-called *intersexuality*, and many more exist than the
individuals affected actually realise themselves. It appears that some individuals
have more and some less chromosomes than the standard 46 (once thought to
be 48). Instead of being either XY (male) or XX (female), there are physically
immature females with one X but no X or Y to partner it, and there are XXX
and XXXX females with varying levels of femininity. Moreover, there are XXY,
XXXY, XXYY, XXXXY and XYY males with varying levels of masculinity
(Smith, 1997: 124–5). Further research may reveal more complexities to the
perceived binary dualism of the sexes, thus posing further complications to
future census recording.

Genetic factors alone, however, may not be solely responsible for intersexuality. There are many cases of individuals changing sex following alterations
in their hormonal secretion, such as normal males with X and Y chromosomes
who suffer either from (a) a gene defect called 5*a* reductase deficiency, who are
born with female external genitalia, but through increasing secretion of testosterone become 'boys' after puberty, or from (b) another gene defect called
testicular feminisation syndrome, who have all the external characteristics of
women (often apparently attractive enough to become beauty contestants) but
whose bodies are "blind to the male sex hormones that the testes are producing"
and remain infertile (Potts and Short, 1999:63). So gender is at the mercy of our
hormones, maleness being imposed by the secretion of male sex hormones.

In these circumstances, it is not surprising that there is real concern that
chemical pollution may be partly responsible for changes in hormonal secretion.
Endocrine disrupters (e.g. dioxins), so-called 'gender bender chemicals' used by
farmers as pesticides on their lands, penetrate the water supply and may have
some effect upon human hormones and thereby the sex of human populations.
There is already ample evidence of the effects of chemical pollutants on animals,
from polar bears in the Arctic to alligators in tropical swamps, and it appears that
in areas suffering from excessive chemical pollution the problem may have been
seriously underestimated. Future biological research may reveal some unusual
demographic anomalies.

Intersexuality is quite different from *transsexuality*, the desire to change sex,
but it is perhaps not so surprising that the occurrence of intersexuality may not be
unrelated to the considerable recent increase in transgender activities and in
transsexuality. Although still relatively rare, the incidence of male-to-female

transsexual operations is increasing, at least in the West; many thousands of such operations are said to have taken place in both the United Kingdom and the United States.

Another cause of inaccuracy in the statistics of males and females is that in many countries population enumeration is not very efficient. For example, national censuses do not always include members of the armed forces, prisoners, diplomats, foreign students or overseas workers, all of which categories usually involve more men than women. Although not numerically important, in some countries there has also been some misreporting of boys as girls in order to escape military service or evil spirits.

Much more important statistically is the census under-enumeration of one sex. This occurs among younger males in many Western countries, some of whom wish for a variety of reasons to evade the attention of the authorities and will thus avoid enumeration at any price. Such is increasingly the case for numerous illegal immigrants and ethnic minorities, as for example in the United States, Canada and in many West European countries. Substantial male under-enumeration has also long been true for the Afro-American population of the United States.

> **Britain** experienced major under-enumeration during the 1991 census, when it is estimated that 1,055,000 people, mostly men aged 15–45 living in the largest cities, escaped enumeration largely because of their political opposition to the unpopular and short-lived 'poll tax', but among many others escaping enumeration were asylum-seekers, anarchists, abandoned Asian women, criminals and sex-workers. It amounted to a 2.2% under-enumeration, but as many as a tenth of all men aged 25–29, thus greatly affecting reported age-specific sex ratios for that census. Of course, post-enumeration checks enable adjustments to be made to the reported sex ratios. Not surprisingly, large numbers are also missing from British official registers.

1.8   Millions of 'Missing Females'

Much more serious numerically and socially is the huge under-enumeration of girls and women in some parts of the world, leading to a phenomenon of 'missing females' that is made worse by their high rates of mortality in some of the more populous LDCs particularly in South and East Asia, where women have long had relatively low status, suffered from relative neglect and have often not been enumerated because of seclusion or privacy of the household. This shortage of enumerated females has become an international demographic scandal, and in the countries concerned it has been highlighted from time to time in the media as the problem of the 'missing women'. The aggregate sex ratio of the LDCs as a whole is very much affected by many tens of millions of these so-called missing women and missing girls who are unaccounted for in official statistics. There can be no precise figure, and certainly estimates vary greatly. Although shortages of enumerated women are widespread in LDCs, they are especially large in the more populous Asian countries of China, India, Pakistan and Bangladesh. It is certainly one of the reasons why United Nations *Demographic Yearbooks* have not provided sex ratios for individual countries, giving only rounded figures for the major world regions.

The main question which has been addressed by demographers is whether the shortage of females results from under-enumeration or from high female mortality. Using country census data for the period 1981–91, the distinguished American demographer Ansley Coale (1991) calculated numbers of females missing in these countries and in Nepal and West Asia by comparing actual and expected sex ratios, and he came to the conclusion that about 60 million females were 'missing' in these countries at that time (see Table 1.1). This is perhaps equivalent to a total approaching 100 million by the year 2000, given the relatively high rates of population growth in some of those countries. Coale largely accounted for the enormous problem of 'missing women' by their differential treatment, in which they receive poorer nutrition and less health care than men.

Obviously, the numbers are merely estimates, and of course the problem is not confined to the countries examined by Coale, for it is certain that it extends to other populous LDCs such as Indonesia, Morocco, Philippines, Taiwan and Turkey. The subject is now receiving a great deal of governmental attention, particularly in China and India, where the whole issue has become politically sensitive. In India alone, more recent estimates of 'missing girls and women' have been of 31.85 million (Agnihotri, 1995) and 35–90 million (Drèze and Sen, 1995).

The phenomenon of missing girls and women itself is not in dispute in those parts of the world, but there are various explanations, which act to a greater or lesser degree in combination, including the following:

- the under-reporting of female births and of females in general,
- the occurrence of female infanticide, abandonment and adoption,

Table 1.1 'Missing Women' in some Asian Countries and Egypt (after Coale)

Country/Region		M/F Ratio		No. of Females	Females Missing	
		Actual	*Expected*	*Millions*	*Per cent*	*Millions*
China	1990	1.006	1.01	548.7	5.3	29.1
India	1991	1.077	1.02	406.3	5.6	22.8
Pakistan	1981	1.105	1.025	40	7.8	3.1
Bangladesh	1981	1.064	1.025	42.2	3.8	1.6
Nepal	1985	1.05	1.025	7.3	2.7	0.2
West Asia	1985	1.06	1.03	55	3	1.7
Egypt	1986	1.047	1.02	23.5	2.6	0.6

Source: Coale, 1991: 522.

- the increasing incidence of sex-selective abortions,
- the occurrence of female neglect, and
- demographically unusual excess female mortality, including high maternal mortality.

These explanations are all accepted as contributory factors to the phenomenon of missing girls and women, but they vary in significance from country to country. Inevitably, statistical evidence for them is sketchy and uneven, and most explanations rely on demographic analysis of secondary data. That is not helped by the fact that in some of these countries the situation is probably better now than in the past and in other countries it is worse.

In **Pakistan**, which has the highest sex ratio of the major populous countries of Asia, the sex ratio apparently declined substantially from over 122 in 1921 and 1931 to approximately 109 today. The improvement is regarded as resulting mainly from a better coverage of females in more recent censuses and the lowering of female mortality in comparison with males, and the sex ratio is expected to fall further (Rukanuddin and Farooqui, 1988: 32).

In contrast, in **India** the sex ratio seems to have risen rather irregularly during much of this century, from 103 in 1901 to 108 in 1991, a level now only just below that of Pakistan – although we should remind ourselves that in the Indian censuses the sex ratios were expressed as 972 and 929 females per thousand males respectively. Indian census officials earlier this century used to attribute the shortage of females to undercounting, but that would not appear to explain the rising sex ratio. The general opinion has been that it is likely to be more attributable to differential mortality arising from the neglect of girls and women and discrimination against them, a topic that will be examined in chapter 4. However, from analysis of the rise of the sex ratio during 1901–91, Peter Mayer (1999: 337) concluded that "discrimination and the differing values placed on women's labour make a relatively minor direct contribution to the historical trend in India's sex ratio", but "have been significant causes of lags in improvement in women's life expectancy; they appear to have established patterns that have been greatly amplified by the demographic transition through which India is now passing". Consequently, he suggested "that it is not appropriate to use sex ratios or trends in sex ratios as indicators of women's relative position in society", but we "should rely instead upon direct measures of education, employment, mortality, life expectancy, and so forth".

We shall examine the various explanations for the missing millions of females more fully in later chapters on the preponderance of male births and deaths.

CHAPTER 2

PATTERNS OF SEX RATIOS

2.1 The World Picture

Given the caveats in the previous chapter concerning doubts about the accuracy of data, the sex ratio of the world population does not seem to vary greatly over time, but according to UN estimates, during the second half of the twentieth century it appears to have risen gradually, from 99.7 males per 100 females in 1950 to 101.5 in 1995 (see Table 2.1), when, according to aggregated national data, 2865 million males outnumbered 2822 million females by about 43 million, almost equivalent to the population of England (United Nations,1999).

Accepting that such figures can only give a broad indication of the gradual rise in the average sex ratio of the world population since mid-century, perhaps the main reason is the recent improvement in the survival of males in the MDCs, partly because the effects of the slaughter of the Second World War have diminished. Thus it appears that the overall sex ratio of MDCs has risen fairly substantially from 91.0 in 1950 to 94.4 in 1995, of course still leaving males markedly outnumbered by females, mostly because of the even better survival rates of females. In contrast, the sex ratio of the much larger aggregate population of the LDCs, now accounting for nearly 80% of the world total, declined

Table 2.1   Male/Female Sex Ratios of the World, MDCs and LDCs, 1950–95

	1950	1970	1985	1995
WORLD	99.7	100.4	101.2	101.5
MDCs	91	93	94.2	94.4
LDCs	104.3	103.5	103.7	103.2

Source: United Nations, *Demographic Yearbooks.*

15

16   *Human Dichotomy*

slightly from 104.3 in 1950 to 103.2 in 1995, still showing a clear surplus of males and reflecting the relatively more difficult living conditions for females.

2.2 Continental and Cultural Variations

Continental variations in sex ratios are greater than global variations over time. They result mainly but not exclusively from differences in the process of mortality decline and its subsequent effects upon the age structures of populations, along with substantial undercounting of females, particularly in Asia. In 1995, continental sex ratios ranged from 93 in Europe and 97 in Northern America, through 99 in both Latin America and Africa and 101 in Oceania, to 105 in Asia. So there is a marked contrast between the male shortages in the more developed continents of Europe and North America and the apparent female shortages in the greater part of the most populous and generally less developed continent of Asia (see Table 2.2). Among the sub-continental regions

Table 2.2   Estimated Populations (in millions) and Sex Ratios of the Major Areas and Regions of the World, 1995

Major Area and Region	Both Sexes	Males	Females	Sex Ratio
World Total	**5687**	**2865**	**2822**	*102*
Africa	**719**	**359**	**361**	**99**
Eastern Africa	221	110	111	99
Middle Africa	83	41	42	98
Northern Africa	158	80	78	101
Southern Africa	47	24	23	104
Western Africa	209	104	105	99
Latin America	**477**	**237**	**240**	**99**
Caribbean	36	18	18	100
Central America	123	61	62	98
South America	317	157	160	98
Northern America	**297**	**146**	**150**	**97**
Asia	**3438**	**1758**	**1680**	**105**
Eastern Asia	1421	728	693	105
South Central Asia	1367	703	664	106
South Eastern Asia	482	240	242	99
Western Asia	168	86	82	105
Europe	**728**	**351**	**377**	**93**
Eastern Europe	311	147	163	90
Northern Europe	93	46	48	96
Southern Europe	143	70	73	96
Western Europe	181	88	93	95
Oceania	**28.3**	**14.2**	**14.1**	*101*
Australia & New Zealand	21.4	10.7	10.7	99
Melanesia	5.8	2.8	2.8	106
Micronesia	0.5	0.2	0.2	107
Polynesia	0.6	0.3	0.3	108

Source: United Nations (1999) *Demographic Yearbook 1997*, 96–7.

the contrasts in sex ratios in 1995 are even greater, with on the one hand an exceptionally low ratio in Eastern Europe (90), well below other regions, and on the other hand high ratios in Eastern Asia (105), Western Asia (105), Central South Asia (106) and in the very small populations of the Pacific island groups. These sharp contrasts will concern us closely in later chapters.

Many of the continental variations in sex ratios reflect far broader demographic differences between the population compositions and dynamics of the world's main civilisations, each based on separate religions and cultures and incorporating hundreds of millions of people: Chinese, Hindu, Islamic, Western, Orthodox, Latin American and Japanese (Huntington, 1996). In focusing on the populations of states, for which data are so much more readily available, demographers have to some extent neglected the very significant demographic distinctiveness of these civilisations. Although China, India and Japan are the core countries of three of these civilisations, the others have no comparable core countries and overlap numerous political boundaries, especially the Western and Islamic civilisations, and hence pose problems of statistical aggregation. Nevertheless, we shall see that these civilisations have a profound influence upon many aspects of population composition and dynamics, including the relative status and numbers of males and females.

2.3   National Variations

There is much more variation of sex ratios at national level than at continental level, not only because we are dealing with populations ranging from a few thousand to more than 1.25 billion, but also because migration plays a much greater role in population change. Excluding those countries with small populations of less than one million inhabitants, the range of sex ratios of the 143 countries shown in Table 2.3 is from 85 to 192. Putting to one side the issue of under-reporting of one sex or the other, the sex ratios of the great majority of countries fall broadly within the range 96-104 males per 100 females, i.e. 4% above or below equal numbers, the United Kingdom coming towards the bottom of that range at 96. The median and modal sex ratio of these countries appears to be 98 males per 100 females, with thirty countries having this ratio, at least for the time being. It is well below the world average of 101.5, largely because several very populous Asian countries (e.g. Bangladesh, China, India and Pakistan) have very high sex ratios of 105 or more.

Small countries with populations well below a million often have very marked surpluses of either males or females, but their sex ratios are more volatile to sudden demographic changes. On the other hand, we should remember that the majority of the world's countries have less than 5 million inhabitants. Although the definition of a country is not easy (does it have to be independent? should it be of a certain size?), the latest population counts of 138 of the 238 countries listed in the United Nations Demographic Yearbook 1997 were less than 5 million; their combined populations only amounted to that of Brazil, the country with the fifth largest population after China, India, United States and Indonesia.

Given the fact that these ratios are estimates and ever changing, one must not read too much into the subtle differences between countries, but Figure 2.1 indicates that the world patterns of sex ratios, here classified simply into four broad categories, do not form a patchwork but tend to mass into large groupings that reflect many of the sub-continental cultural groupings previously mentioned. Viewed along with Table 2.3, it will be seen that a long belt of Central Asian, East European, Central European and some West European countries stretching from Russia and Kazakhstan in the east to France and Portugal in the

Table 2.3   Estimated Sex Ratios of Selected Countries with 1 million inhabitants or more, mid-1990s

85	Ukraine
88	Belarus, Latvia, Russia
89	Estonia
90	Georgia, Lithuania
91	Moldova
92	Botswana
93	Austria, Cambodia, Hungary, Portugal
94	Central African Republic, Croatia, Czech Republic, Finland, Germany, Guinea Bissau, Italy, Kazakhstan, Slovenia
95	Azerbaijan, France, Kyrgyzstan, Lebanon, Namibia, Nicaragua, Poland, Puerto Rico, United States, Uruguay
96	Armenia, Belgium, Bulgaria, Burundi, Congo, El Salvador, Haiti, Slovakia, Switzerland, United Kingdom
97	Angola, Canada, Chad, Greece, Japan, Laos, Mali, North Korea, Sierra Leone, Spain, Sweden, Turkmenistan, Vietnam
98	Argentina, Benin, Bolivia, Burkina Faso, Chile, Colombia, Denmark, Gabon, Israel, Madagascar, Malawi, Mauritania, Mozambique, Netherlands, New Zealand, Niger, Nigeria, Norway, Romania, Rwanda, Somalia, Tanzania, Thailand, Togo, Trinidad and Tobago, Uzbekistan, Yemen, Yugoslavia, Zaire, Zambia
99	Bosnia-Herzegovina, Brazil, Cameroon, Ghana, Indonesia, Mexico, Myanmar, South Africa, Sri Lanka, Tajikistan, Uganda, Zimbabwe
100	Algeria, Australia, Ethiopia, Ireland, Jamaica, Kenya, Morocco, Senegal
101	Cuba, Ecuador, Eritrea, Guinea, Peru, Sudan, Venezuela
102	Costa Rica, Guatemala, Honduras, Liberia, Macedonia, Malaysia, Paraguay, South Korea, Syria, Tunisia
103	Dominican Republic, Egypt, Iran, Ivory Coast, Kuwait, Panama, Philippines, Singapore
104	Iraq, Turkey
105	Afghanistan, Albania, China, Jordan, Nepal
106	Bangladesh, Taiwan
108	India
109	Libya, Pakistan
123	Saudi Arabia
192	United Arab Emirates

Source of data: Neft and Levine, 1997: 7–8.

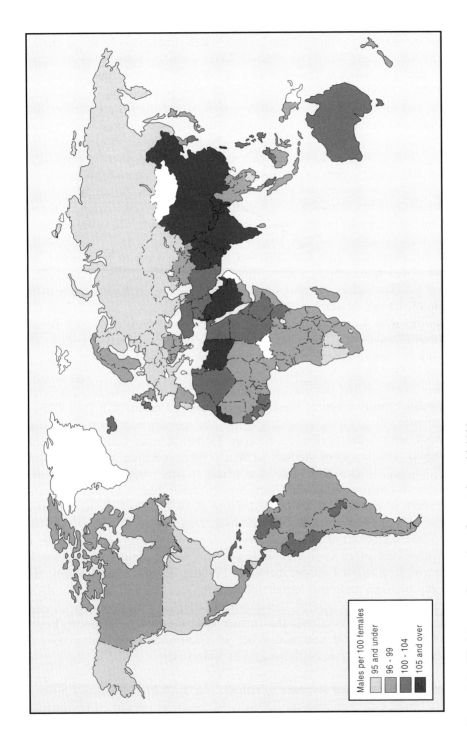

Figure 2.1 World map of sex ratios of countries. mid-1990s.

west clearly experience the lowest sex ratios of 95 and under. It may also be said to cross the Atlantic to include the United States, and countries to the north and south in Europe and North America all have sex ratios below 100. At the other end of the scale, there is a similar belt of more or less contiguous East Asian, South Asian, South West Asian and North African countries, including many Muslim and oil-rich Middle Eastern countries, stretching from China in the east to Mauritania in the west all experiencing sex ratios of 100 and over, and often of 105 or more. Malaysia and Australia creep in as outliers along with a few countries in Latin America (e.g. Peru and Venezuela). Most other countries fall into the intermediate category with sex ratios of 96–99, again fairly contiguously in Latin America, Southern Europe, Sub-Saharan Africa, South West Asia and South East Asia but also including Japan, Canada and New Zealand. Of course, there are anomalies to these geographical groupings, both above and below, but the patterns stand out.

The countries with low and high sex ratios also tend to fall loosely into a number of different categories according to explanatory factors (Noin, 1991: 50), but it must be emphasised that these are not discrete and sometimes overlap, because the causes of sex ratios are multi-dimensional:

Countries with a marked shortage of males, i.e. with low sex ratios below 95 and sometimes below 90, have been particularly influenced by one or more of the following factors summarised below, and to be explained more fully later:

- *Recent conflicts and wars* causing large military losses, as for example the twentieth century cases of Cambodia and many Central and East European countries such as Germany, Austria and the western republics of the former Soviet Union (Ukraine, Russia, Belarus, Estonia, Latvia, Lithuania, Moldova, Georgia). The impact of the Second World War on Russia was massive and its effects persist to this day, in great contrast to other European countries like Sweden and Switzerland, which were largely unaffected; in 1959 the sex ratio of the whole Soviet Union was only 81.9 and in 1950 that of the Soviet Zone of Germany was even lower at 80.2 (Shryock, Siegel *et al.*, 1973).
- *Unusually high levels of male mortality*, as occur particularly at the present time in Russia and other former republics of the Soviet Union along with other countries in Eastern Europe, including Finland, Poland and Hungary, where the gap between male and female life expectancy is widest; and
- *Emigration of men*, which has had important effects on the demography of such countries as Italy, Portugal, the former East Germany, Lebanon, Lesotho, Botswana, Swaziland and a number of Caribbean islands (e.g. Grenada, Barbados, Puerto Rico, St. Kitts and St Vincent).

Countries with a marked shortage of females, i.e. with high sex ratios often over 105, are found especially in a mixed array of countries influenced by the following demographic characteristics:

- *Immigration of men*, such as in the sometimes small and often sparsely populated oil-rich states of the Gulf (Qatar, Bahrain, United Arab Emirates, Saudi Arabia, Oman, Kuwait) and elsewhere (e.g. Libya, Brunei) which have undergone rapid economic and demographic growth;
- *Emigration of women*, as from Ireland in the past, the Philippines today and some of the smaller populations of the Pacific islands (e.g. Guam, Fiji, Solomon Islands), where work opportunities for women are few; and
- *Unusually high female mortality*, that has been common in many Asian countries like India, Pakistan, Nepal, Bangladesh, as well as in numerous countries of Sub-Saharan Africa.

Variations in national sex ratios have also been associated with many aspects of society, economy and polity. Most commonly they are linked to the employment market and the need for labour. For instance, it is well known that the ageing populations of MDCs, with increasing proportions of elderly women, have attracted large inflows of young workers from other countries that are less developed, a topic that we shall look at in Chapter 5.

Rather more questionably, variations in national sex ratios have been regarded as affecting a number of other national characteristics, such as an excess of males encouraging militaristic aims and a shortage leading to military weakness.

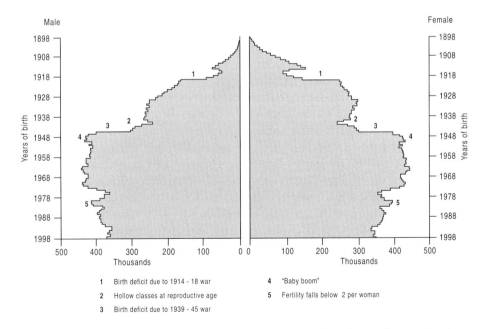

1	Birth deficit due to 1914 - 18 war	4	"Baby boom"
2	Hollow classes at reproductive age	5	Fertility falls below 2 per woman
3	Birth deficit due to 1939 - 45 war		

Figure 2.2 The age pyramid of France, 1999, showing the hollow classes. *Source: Population*, 1999, 54(3), 465.

Exemplifying the latter case, ***France*** during the inter-war years was regarded
by many, both internally and externally, as militarily vulnerable because of
its dearth of young men after the devastation of the First World War
(Dyer, 1978). During that war it suffered 1.7 million war deaths, 13.2%
of the active male population, as well as a substantial reduction in the
number of births, so that the total population deficit of the war was roughly
3 million people, causing gaps in the population pyramid – *les classes
creuses* or hollow classes – which are still visible in the population pyramid
and emphasising the growing proportion of old people, especially old
women (see Figure 2.2). Consequently, in 1921 France's overall sex ratio
was 91, which only rose to 93 by 1938 because of the influx of millions of
male immigrant workers from Italy, Poland, Spain, Belgium and elsewhere
to work in many of the country's basic industries, many of which were
located vulnerably near to its borders; in 1927, 42% of the coal miners in
France were foreign (particularly Poles) and they were mainly in the northern coalfield along the Belgian border. The overall demographic situation
contrasted most strikingly with that prevailing in France's fascist neighbours, Germany and Italy, which had implemented populationist policies
to swell their numbers rapidly. While the respective numbers of young men
aged 20–34 in France and Germany at the time of the Franco-Prussian War
in 1870 were 4.4 and 4.9 million, at the beginning of the Second World War
in 1939 the relative numbers were 4.3 and 9.4 million. This was seen to be a
factor behind German aggression and was a cause for great concern in
France at the time. There was much pessimistic talk of depopulation and
population decline, so the government was stimulated to introduce policies
to protect the family and encourage larger families. It also created a
National Institute of Demographic Studies (INED), that became inter-
nationally famous and had long-term effects on the study of population.
Despite the losses and birth deficit in the Second World War, these policies
subsequently helped the remarkable and unforeseen demographic revival of
France during the second half of the twentieth century when its population
rose from 40 million to nearly 60 million. This was also facilitated by further
immigration, especially of men from overseas territories during the first few
post-war decades, which helped to make up for losses among the younger
adults, so that the overall sex ratio rose to 96 by 1975 (Noin and Chauviré,
1987: 59–61). Foreigners lifted the sex ratio; in 1982, there were 2.10 million
males in the 3.68 million foreign population and the sex ratios of their age
groups 35–55 were 200 or more (Ogden and Winchester, 1986). Thereafter,
immigration has been more balanced, and along with the increasing ageing
of the population, leading especially to more elderly women, the sex ratio
settled down during the 1980s and 1990s to about 95, approximately the
average for Western Europe.

Another perceived effect of sex ratios is that they have been commonly associated with marriage rates in countries, any shortage of marriageable males or females producing a 'marriage squeeze' (Eshleman, 2000). An investigation of 111 countries showed that the higher the sex ratios the higher the proportion of women who marry and the younger they do so (South, 1988). And in a sample study of 66 countries, high sex ratios (i.e. an under-supply of women) have been seen to be one of four factors affecting high divorce rates, the others being late marriage of women, level of socio-economic development and female labour force participation rates (Trent and South, 1989).

Sex ratios have also been linked with types of marriage practices prevailing in different countries. Monogamous marriage has been seen as essentially a pairing and coupling of men and women, and in many societies it has been a nearly universal phenomenon that has been dependent on fairly equal numbers of men and women. But in the majority of traditional societies monogamy has been far from being the only marriage practice, polygamy being also allowed, particularly polygyny (having more than one wife at the same time); polyandry (having more than one husband at the same time) is very much rarer and found only in a few cultures (e.g. the Todas of India and the Yanomama of Brazil). With monogamy becoming increasingly the most common form of marriage, it has been suggested that large-scale polygamy is only possible where there are unbalanced sex ratios (Eshleman, 2000: 46). Of course, they may have some influence on the marriage market locally and lead to some exogamy (marrying outside the social unit), but widespread exogamy, as occurring in India and accounting for much short-distance migration there, is unlikely to be induced by demography alone.

Moreover, statistical evidence for polygamous marriage practices being primarily influenced by sex ratios is not readily forthcoming at the country level. Certainly, many countries where polygyny is commonly practised, as in Sub-Saharan Africa (Brass *et al.*, 1968; Hertrich and Locoh, 1999), do not currently have very high sex ratios. For example, it is widespread to a greater or lesser extent over much of West Africa, but the region's average sex ratio is 99 – middle of the range. In Togo the sex ratio is 98, yet over half of all married women are said to be in polygynous relationships (Neft and Levine, 1997: 94–5), and in Mali, Nigeria and Senegal, where over 40% of married women are polygynous, the sex ratios are 97, 98 and 100 respectively, not unusual enough to indicate the necessity for so much polygyny at the present time. No doubt polygyny was to some extent influenced by the very different demographic situation which prevailed in West Africa during the sixteenth to nineteenth centuries, when millions of slaves were shipped to the Americas, when millions were enslaved to work within Africa itself, when millions of others lost their lives in the barbaric process of slavery, and when the appalling indigenous practices of human sacrifice also wreaked havoc in some kingdoms, as for example Dahomey and Asante (see Reader, 1997: 399–459). Such practices have fortunately disappeared, but their influence upon cultural customs remains, and polygyny seems to take place more in accordance with those customs than as a result of any current demographic imperative. The prevalence of the practice of post-partum sexual abstinence in many African societies is certainly a factor related to polygyny (Page and Lestaeghe, 1981).

On the other hand, there is a case for saying that serial monogamy, or successive monogamous marriage, a practice that has become common in many modern societies as for example in the United States where the multiple marriages of many film stars are much publicised, is facilitated (but not caused) by the growing surplus of women among the older age groups. In the Western world, as we shall see, demography makes remarriage much easier for older men.

2.4 Regional Variations

In some large populous countries, major regional differences in cultures and societies are reflected in diverse regional patterns of sex ratios in which sex-differentials in fertility and mortality both play a significant part, apart from the pervasive influence of migration. For example, the north and south of India and the east and west of China exhibit contrasting sex ratios associated with substantially different cultural traditions and demographic characteristics.

A relevant factor in ***India*** is the influence of religion and its associated customs: since 1931 at least, Christians in southern India have had lower than average sex ratios, Hindus (who constitute the vast majority of the population) have had about average ratios, while in the north Sikhs have had by far the highest ratios followed by Muslims (United Nations, 1982: 78–80). But the situation is more complicated, for in broad terms southern Peninsular India has also progressed further through the demographic transition than northern India of the Indo-Gangetic Plain. In the south, the status of women is generally much higher and sex ratios are much lower, and thus most of the 10% of Indian districts where females out-number males are in the south-west and in the tribal belt of central India. At the state level, even substantial boundary changes during the twentieth century do not obscure the considerable variations in sex ratio (see Table 2.4), which were larger at the beginning of the century than the end (Bittles *et al.*, 1993). The southern state of Kerala, which has by far the highest UN human development index (UNFPA, 1997) and levels of male and female literacy, is alone in having had more females than males throughout the twentieth century with a sex ratio of 99.6 in 1901 and 96.5 in 1991 (or, using the Indian method of expressing sex ratios, 1036 females per 1000 males), although several other states and union territories (e.g. Tamil Nadu,

Table 2.4   Twentieth Century Changes in Sex Ratios of Indian States and Union Territories

STATE or Union Territory	1901	1931	1961	1991
Northern Zone				
Chandigarh	–	–	–	126.6
DELHI	116	138.5	127.4	120.9
HARYANA	–	–	–	115.6
HIMACHAL PRADESH	113	110.4	108.4	102.5
JAMMU & KASHMIR	113.4	115.6	114	–
PUNJAB	117.9*	120.5*	115.7*	113.4
RAJASTHAN	110.5	110.3	110.1	109.9
Central Zone				
MADHYA PRADESH	101	102.7	105	107.4
UTTAR PRADESH	106.7	110.7	110	113.8
Eastern Zone				
Andaman & Nicobar	314	201.8	168.1	122.2
ARUNACHAL PRADESH	–	–	111.9	116.4
ASSAM	107.2^	112.9^	114.9^	108.3
BIHAR	94.8	100.7	100.6	109.8
MANIPUR	96.4	93.9	98.5	104.4
MEGHALAYA	–	–	–	104.7
MIZORAM	–	–	–	108.6
NAGALAND	102.8	100.3	107.2	112.9
ORISSA	96.4	93.7	99.9	103
SIKKIM	109.1	103.4	110.2	113.9
TRIPURA	114.4	113	107.5	103.8
WEST BENGAL	105.8	112.3	113.9	109.1
Western Zone				
Dadra & Nagar Haveli	104.1	109.7	103.8	105
Daman & Diu	–	–	–	103.2
GOA	92.7″	92.2″	93.5″	103.4
GUJARAT	104.8	105.8	106.4	107.1
MAHARASHTRA	102.2	105.6	106.8	107.1
Southern Zone				
ANDHRA PRADESH	101.5	101.4	101.9	102.9
KERALA	99.6	97.9	97.9	96.5
KARNATAKA	101.7	103.6	104.3	104.2
Lakshadweep	94	100.6	98	106
Pondicherry	–	–	98.7	102.1
TAMIL NADU	95.8	97.3	100.8	102.7
ALL INDIA	**102.9**	**105.3**	**106.3**	**107.9**

Source: United Nations, 1982 and UNFPA, 1997.
Notes: * Includes Haryana and Chandigarh. ^ Includes Meghalaya. ″ Includes Daman and Diu.

Pondicherry, Lakshadweep, Goa, Manipur and Orissa) have known periods of female preponderance. In sharp contrast, high sex ratios and shortages of females have persisted over all states of northern and central India (e.g. Punjab, Haryana, Madhya Pradesh, Rajasthan and Uttar Pradesh) where the status of women and UN human development indices are very much lower. At district level the map of Indian sex ratios (Figure 2.3) becomes

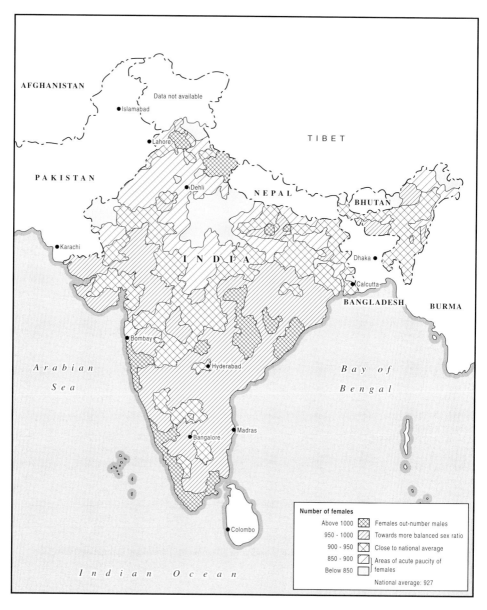

Figure 2.3 Map of contrasting sex ratios in northern and southern India, 1991, using the Inidian practice of expressing sex ratios as females per 1000 males. *Source*: *Population Geography*, 1994, 16(1&2), Map 3.

more complicated as it reflects many cultural, economic and demographic phenomena, in particular the effects of migration (Atkins *et al.*, 1997; Kumar *et al.*, 1997).

MDCs are not excluded from regional contrasts in sex ratios that have been caused by ethnic, religious and cultural differences affecting differential life expectancy. They may help to explain, for example, the unusually low sex ratios in Galicia compared with the rest of Spain, and the lower sex ratios of the more ageing populations living in the west and south of France compared with those in the north and east where there are more industrial centres and where most of the immigrants live (Noin and Chauviré, 1987: 60–1).

Using standardised masculinity ratios, Decroly and Vanlaer (1991: 127–32) were able to show the complex patterns of sex structures in the whole of Europe for 1960 and 1980, the causes of which are varied. At one end of the scale were the very low standardised ratios (below 90 and even below 80 in some districts) over nearly all of the European part of the former Soviet Union, East Germany and parts of West Germany (e.g. Bavaria) and Poland, all greatly affected by heavy losses of men during the Second World War and continuing to experience high male mortality. In the Autonomous Republic of Mariyskaya in the east of European Russia the standardised ratio was as low as 68 in 1960 and 76 in 1980. In some oblasts of central Russia and northern Ukraine in 1960 there were 3–4 times as many women as men aged 70 or more. In addition, very low ratios were found in parts of Romania, southern Finland and in northern Portugal, the latter affected especially by emigration. At the other end of the scale were the very high ratios found over most of Norway, Sweden, Denmark, Eire, Albania, Macedonia and to a rather more limited extent over much of France and northern Spain, all less affected by war and more affected by emigration and ageing of populations. They reached a peak in County Leitrim in north-west Eire with standardised sex ratios of 117 in 1960 and 115 in 1980. Some of the subtle variations in regional sex ratios in Western Europe in 1997 can be seen in Figure 2.4.

In the former ***Federal Republic of Yugoslavia***, the northern republics of Slovenia and Croatia long experienced lower sex ratios than the southern republics of Serbia and Macedonia, largely because women have fared better there and lived longer. And before the recent conflicts and demographic upheavals in Yugoslavia, Youssef Courbage (1991) noted differences in female mortality even among the Muslim populations of Yugoslavia; the less modernised Albanian women of Kosovo who had preserved more traditional Mediterranean customs experienced higher mortality rates than Bosnian women, whose customs have been closer to those of the Serbs and Croats. The political turmoil in the Balkans during the 1990s has of course totally altered the previous demographic patterns.

Human Dichotomy

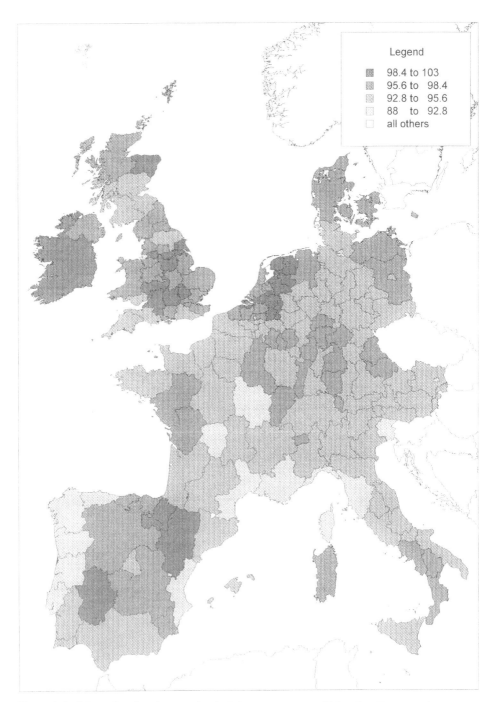

Figure 2.4 Map of regional sex ratios in Western Europe, 1997, using Eurostat data. *Source*: r-cade, University of Durham.

In most countries the main cause of regional variations in sex ratios is differential migration, which has effects upon regional patterns as well as on urban-
rural contrasts. Migration has had a major impact on the spread of colonisation
of countries and on the changing patterns of settlement. The process of colonisation of frontier regions by conquest, clearance and economic development has
always initially involved more men than women, whether in the remote past or
in recent centuries. Thus, very imbalanced sex ratios have been found along the
frontier fringes, as in the case of the colonisation of the United States, Canada,
Australia, New Zealand, South America, South Africa and Russia during the
eighteenth and nineteenth centuries, especially where mining was involved, and
these imbalances persisted to some extent for many decades.

During the push west of the American frontier, for example, the western
states of the **United States** long had extremely high sex ratios (and very
male-dominated societies) whereas those in the east and south had much
lower ratios, and although these differences were attenuated with every
subsequent census they were still detectable during the early decades of
the twentieth century (Thompson and Lewis, 1965: 73–84). In 1850, the
sex ratio of the region of the West was 278.9 (it was as high as 778.5 in
its Pacific division – no wonder the West was wild!) compared with only
101.2 in the Northeast region, which traditionally has had the most
balanced sex ratios. Gold rushes played a major role in the high sex ratios
of the West, and in the latter part of the nineteenth century the sex ratios of
the Chinese and Japanese populations of the United States, which were
mostly localised in the West, both exceeded 2000, largely because females
were not allowed to join them. By 1900 the respective regional figures for
the West and Northeast had fallen to 128.1 and 100.0; but by 1950 they
were down to 102.1 and 96.1, less than three points different from that of
the United States as a whole (98.6).

In **Canada**, the decline in sex ratios of the country as a whole and
in particular of its western provinces was slower, possibly because of
their persistant reliance on primary production but also their harsher
climatic environment. In 1911, when Canada's sex ratio was 113 that of
the prairie province of Alberta was still as high as 149. Although both
ratios fell gradually during the twentieth century, Canada's ratio did not
fall below 100 until 1971, and Alberta's has not yet done so.

Australia's gold rushes, particularly to Victoria, Western Australia and
Queensland during the period 1851–1911, also led to some very distorted
patterns of sex ratios (Rowland, 1979: 17–21). A census in 1857 revealed
that on the goldfields of Victoria there were about 44,143 women and
102,285 men, giving a sex ratio of 232 much higher than the already high
figure of 163 for the state of Victoria as a whole, which was then at a
pioneering stage. Even more remarkable was the fact that only three of

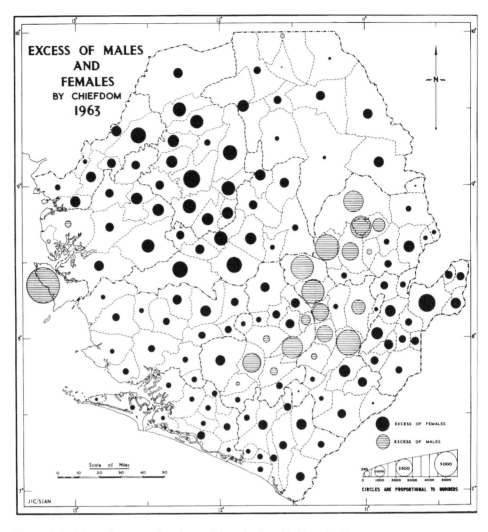

Figure 2.5 Map of excess of males and females by chiefdom in Sierra Leone, 1963. *Source:* Clarke, 1966, 44–5.

the 25,424 Chinese inhabitants of Victoria in 1857 were women, mainly because the Chinese came as sojourners intending to return home when they had made their fortunes. The sex ratios in the Western Australian goldfields in 1901 resembled those of Victoria in 1857, but the pattern was not confined to goldfields; a much later mining rush for base metals during 1966–71 led to even higher sex ratios in the Pilbara where the sex ratio was 271 in 1971 (Rowland, 1979: 39).

About the same time, *Sierra Leone* was one of several African countries that demonstrated the clear impact of alluvial diamond mining on the distribution of males and females. The 1963 census revealed that 19 chiefdoms of the diamond areas of Kono, Kenema and Bo districts in eastern Sierra Leone had an excess of over 46,000 males (Figure 2.5), through attracting large numbers of male adult migrant workers especially from the northern part of the country, where the people had higher fertility but their region had limited economic opportunity and low agricultural potential (Clarke, 1966; Swindell, 1970). The other concentration of males marked on Figure 2.5 was the Western Area, which incorporated the capital and main city, Freetown. Of course, the civil war which tragically tore the country apart in the later years of the twentieth century transformed the demographic patterns and caused massive flights of refugees.

The above examples refer particularly to the early stages in the evolution of mining, when men play the primordial roles, but as mining communities become well established the sex ratios become less unbalanced. Thus, the coalfields in Western Europe, which had such a marked effect upon the map of population distribution during the nineteenth and twentieth centuries especially through their attraction of associated heavy industries, were not clearly visible on the maps of sex ratios of 1960 and 1980 (Decroly and Vanlaer, 1991: 127–32). During their decline and frequent eventual demise, many older miners retired and stayed in their communities, so even the 50-year decline of employment in coalmining in Britain from 704,000 in 1947 to 8,000 in 1997 had less impact upon the map of sex ratios than might be imagined.

2.5   Rural-Urban Variations

Migration has not only expanded settlement; it has also helped to create the growing concentration of population on relatively small areas of the earth's surface. In particular, it has contributed greatly to the evolution of specialised economic regions, notably economic core regions, and to the massive growth of towns and cities, the two processes of population redistribution invariably being coincidental. Over the last two centuries migration has played a very important role in the astonishingly rapid process of urbanisation which has resulted in an immense shift in global population distribution, affecting almost all countries, and this process has greatly affected the distribution of males and females.

Stimulated primarily by the rise of capitalism and its spatial effects, the proportion of the world's population living in towns has increased phenomenally from less than 3% of one billion people in 1800, to just under 30% of 2.5 billion in 1950, to nearly half of over 6 billion in 2000 (50% will probably be attained in 2006), and it is expected to rise to almost three-fifths of over 8 billion in 2030, when the urban population is projected to reach 5.1 billion (United Nations, 1998). About 90% of the world's population growth will have taken place in towns and cities. Like most of the world's population growth, most of this urban growth will have taken place in LDCs, many of which have undergone massive socio-economic transformations from rural agricultural societies to urban industrial and service societies. Precision in percentages is once again difficult, as definitions of urban vary greatly from country to country and as the linear spatial boundary between what is urban and what is rural is so often indeterminate. There is, however, no doubting the importance of urbanisation within a large number of economic core areas, which are mostly concentrated along the coastal fringes of the continents, where the new global economic order functions most, involving the transnationalisation of production and the international service economy.

The main foci have been the mega-city-ports that are the gateways to countries in close contact with the rest of the global economy. In 1950, New York was the only city with more than ten million inhabitants; by 1995, there were 14, ten of them in LDCs. Mega-cities in LDCs are often outgrowing in population if not in functions many of the major cities of the more developed world, but growth rates are variable, less because of attempts to slow their growth and more because of the decline in some national population growth rates. The fastest growing mega-cities are those within countries with rapid population growth. Thus, while Dhaka grew by 7.7% per annum during 1975–95 and Lagos by 5.8%, Shanghai grew by only 0.9% per annum and Rio de Janeiro and Buenos Aires by 1.3% (United Nations, 1998).

Because a considerable part of the process of urbanisation has resulted from rural-urban migration, it has had a profound but uneven impact upon the redistribution of males and females within countries. In LDCs the effects are certainly not uniform (Gugler, 1997), as urban sex ratios also reflect the youthfulness of populations containing many young males. In much of Latin America (e.g. Brazil, Chile, Colombia, Ecuador, Mexico and Peru), one of the most urbanised regions of the developing world, the migration of women from rural areas to cities, primarily for domestic and service employment, has long been very important and has had consequent effects upon both urban and rural sex ratios, so that the patterns are more like those of MDCs than LDCs (see Table 2.5). Indeed, contrasts in urban and rural sex ratios in Latin America at the time of the 1960 round of censuses were much greater than today; in a number of countries (e.g. Costa Rica, Chile, El Salvador) urban sex ratios were below 89 while in contrast their rural sex ratios were 104–15 (Clarke, 1971: 71; Findley, 1999). One surprising localised result in the 1990s of the urban concentration of women occurring in the city of Recife in north-east Brazil, which had a surplus of about 100,000 females in a population of 1.3 million, was that it became an attractive long-distance marriage market for lonesome German men, a phenomenon not dissimilar from cities in South East Asia, notably in Thailand and the Philippines. In general, with the exception of Thailand, South East Asian urban sex ratios are rather higher, but they are still lower than the national sex ratios, and the overall levels of urbanisation are much lower than in Latin America.

Table 2.5   National and Urban Sex Ratios and Percentage Urban in Selected MDCs and LDCs, early 1990s

Country, Census Year	National S.R.	Urban S.R.	% Urban
MDCs			
USA, 1990	95.1	94.8	75.2
Canada, 1991	97.2	94.8	76.6
France, 1990	94.8	92.9	74
Greece, 1991	97.1	93.3	58.9
Ireland, 1991	98.9	93.6	57
Spain, 1991	96.2	93.9	64.1
Sweden, 1990	97.5	95.2	83.4
New Zealand, 1991	97.2	94.9	84.9
Japan, 1995	96.2	96.8	78.1
Russian Federation, 1989	87.4	87.3	73.4
LDCs			
Brazil, 1991	97.5	94.3	75.6
Chile, 1992	96.4	92.9	83.5
Colombia	96.9	91.1	71
Ecuador, 1990	98.9	94.5	55.4
Mexico, 1990	96.4	94.7	71.3
Peru, 1993	98.7	96.9	70.1
Malaysia, 1991	101.8	100.7	50.7
Philippines, 1990	101.1	97.7	48.6
Thailand, 1990	98.3	93.8	18.7
China, 1990	106	108.6	26.2
India, 1991	107.9	111.9	25.7
Turkey, 1990	102.7	107.3	59
Tunisia, 1994	102.1	102.7	61
South Africa, 1991	99.8	103.2	56.6
Zambia, 1990	96	100.2	39.4
Uganda, 1991	96.5	94.2	11.3

Source: Gugler, 1997, adapted from UN (1998) *Demographic Yearbook 1996*, UN, New York, and UN (1999) *Demographic Yearbook, 1997*, UN, New York.

The above situation is not the rule, for in many LDCs, especially those in other parts of Asia and in Africa, women have migrated much less to cities, partly because of social constraints but also because of more limited job opportunities for them there. Consequently, urban sex ratios are often higher than national sex ratios, as Table 2.5 reveals in the cases of China, India, Turkey, Tunisia, South Africa and Zambia, but because of increasing rural-urban migration of women they are not as high as they were earlier in the twentieth century. For example, all but one (Sfax) of the 12 largest towns in Tunisia in 1966 had higher sex ratios than the average urban sex ratio of 102.7 in 1991, and the sex ratio of Tunis was 115.0, giving an excess of 32,600 males in a population of 469,000. As to be expected, oil-rich Kuwait City's sex ratio of 158 in 1965 was much more exceptional, but most cities of the Middle East and South Asia were more preponderantly male than they are today (Clarke, 1971; Clarke and Fisher, 1972). In the former East Pakistan (now Bangladesh), the sex ratio of the urban population was 142.2 in 1961, while the rural ratio was 105.9, and some towns, for example Chittagong and Khulna, had twice as many males as females.

> In *India*, the urban sex ratio was consistently higher than the rural sex ratio in all census years and in almost all states during the twentieth century. It rose regularly from 109.9 in 1901 to a peak of 120.4 in 1941, after which it declined irregularly to 111.9 in 1991. The respective figures for Delhi were even higher: 116.0, 139.9 (its peak) and 120.9. The pattern is more or less the same for all states, indicating perhaps that migration to urban centres is now less male-dominated than in the first half of the twentieth century, and involves more families and more women migrating to towns to marry (United Nations, 1982; UNFPA, 1997). Northern states generally have consistently higher urban sex ratios (i.e. 115–30) than southern ones (105 or less) and a greater difference between urban and rural sex ratios, because migration streams include more males. Only the southern state of Kerala consistently recorded an urban sex ratio below 100 during the whole of the twentieth century, it being 96.4 in 1991, more like a European country than an Indian state (Prakash, 1999: 153).

With the notable exception of Ethiopia, urban sex ratios in the countries of Sub-Saharan Africa are generally higher than for countries as a whole, but as many women are migrating more autonomously than in the past the differential is usually diminishing, as in Ghana, Kenya, South Africa, Tanzania and Zimbabwe. In South Africa, for instance, the urban sex ratio declined from 119.2 in 1951 to 103.2 in 1991, at the same time that the national sex ratio declined from 103.1 to 99.8. Broadly, in most MDCs at the time of the 1990 round of censuses both total and urban sex ratios were in the 90s, but total sex ratios were characteristically a few points above the even more female-dominated urban sex ratios (see Table 2.5) reflecting ageing populations and the fact that rural-urban migration in MDCs, at least in recent decades, has mostly involved more women than men with the result that urban areas usually have lower sex ratios than the rural areas. Exceptionally, the urban sex ratios in the former Soviet Union were much lower still; the 1989 census revealed urban sex ratios below 90 in Russia (87.3), Belarus (89.3), Estonia (86.0), Latvia (85.3) and Lithuania (89.1), but these were all not too dissimilar from the very low national sex ratios. Japan's urban sex ratio was also slightly unusual in being marginally higher than the total sex ratio.

> Only in *Ireland*, always out of the ordinary demographically because of the long-term effects of emigration since the mid-nineteenth century, was the total sex ratio of 98.9 in 1991 substantially higher than the urban sex ratio (93.6). This is an indication of the prolonged effect of strong female out-migration from rural Ireland to the main cities and abroad, and the

persistent prevalence of males in the more remote rural areas (Garvey, 1983). However, Ireland is now changing greatly since its membership of the European Community. Its population has risen to 3.6 million in 2000, and the sex ratio pattern is now much less contrasted than it was earlier in the twentieth century, when there was consistent surplus of males and an urban-rural gradient in sex ratios with Dublin having the lowest (e.g. 87.6 in 1951). In 1936, for example, the total sex ratio was as high as that of China today at 105.0 (although like the Indian census it was expressed as 952 females per 1000 males) but the aggregate urban sex ratio was only 90.1, a gap of nearly 15 points, and the rural sex ratio a male-predominant 114.4. Traditional rural households reflected this picture, more than a third of the men aged 45 and over being single, and many of the small farms being run by lone bachelors.

Within the compact living space of **Britain**, as in many other larger MDCs, the distinction between urban and rural is not very clear so that rural-urban migration is not the only form of migration affecting patterns of sex ratios, especially as long-distance commuting and the process of counter-urbanisation to smaller towns are widespread. Rural areas are far from being devoted to purely agricultural activities, although where these activities prevail the sex ratios are often high owing to the greater out-migration of women. In the past many rural areas in Britain were trans-formed by coalfields, where male labour has been dominant, as well as by isolated military establishments, industrial estates, holiday villages, caravan sites and public schools, and they are also used as dormitories and for second homes by people working in towns. All of these factors complicate the local patterns, so that there is no simple pattern of rural sex ratios.

On the whole, urban sex ratios have been more obviously related to urban functions, but single-function towns have dwindled and the diversity of functions has greatly increased, especially by the expansion of those loosely called the service industries. In Britain, the sex ratios of fewer towns reflect the former prominence of male-dominated heavy industries, ports or military establishments or the prominence of female-dominated textile industries. More common has been the diffusion of innumerable light indus-tries and service industries which have been less selective of gender and where female employment has played an increasing and often primordial role. In Britain the demise of the heavy industries of coal mining, shipbuild-ing, steel and to a lesser extent chemicals has been replaced by numerous industrial estates with all manner of small factories and service centres. As a result, some of the patterns and sharp contrasts in urban sex ratios seen in the past (Clarke, 1960) are no longer as vivid. Typical of the 1990s are the mushrooming 'call centres' that employ large numbers of women mostly commuting by car from their village or town of residence. It has been estimated that in 2000 these call centres accounted for between 2–3% of all jobs in the United Kingdom, about 70% taken by women, and they are located mainly in places like Sunderland, Newcastle, Doncaster, Dunfermline, Preston and Warrington, all of which were renowned for male-dominated heavy industries in the past and which are now experiencing massive social change.

2.6   Local Variations

Sex ratios of small populations vary greatly. This is particularly evident when grid square data are analysed, as in the 1971 census of Great Britain when the density of population of the 151,885 inhabited kilometre squares ranged from one individual in some rural areas (the data being suppressed for confidentiality purposes) to 24,286 persons in part of London, with consequent effects upon population structures (Census Research Unit, 1980; Clarke and Rhind, 1976).

Sex ratios may be so unbalanced among small local populations that they provoke social instability or insecurity. Such has been the case in some newly colonised settlements of the 'Wild West', in remote male-dominated, company-owned mining camps, in isolated military bases, in new heavy industrial centres and in many Third World shanty towns. Generally the imbalance declines over time, but much depends on the location and the cultural setting.

The phenomenon of unbalanced local sex ratios is not confined to new settlements. A recent feature of many large cities in MDCs is the great increase in the number of people living alone, especially middle class working women. This growing feminisation of certain quarters of large cities can be seen in both France and Britain; in France as many as 20% of all women professionals live alone, mostly in Paris and the main cities. Of course, the largest concentrations of one-person households are found in capital cities; in 1991, 37% of all households in inner London were of single persons, many of them young women, and in Paris it was 50% (Hall *et al.*, 1997). In addition, many suburban areas have a high proportion of elderly widows living alone, as they find it easier to live in towns than in rural areas because of easier access to facilities and amenities. The coastal resorts of Britain and France have long had some of their countries' lowest sex ratios, where women had settled in retirement with their husbands but outlived them.

The rise in the proportion of one-person households in MDCs is a reflection of the divisive effects of the huge growth in human mobility and of the rapidity of social change, including the decline of family size (both extended and nuclear) and the increase in the frequency of divorce, one-parent families, cohabitation and the elderly living alone, with consequent massive effects upon housing demand and the housing stock. All this is in great contrast with the past, when households were much larger and one-person households very rare. In seventeenth and eighteenth century England, for example, only about 1% of households were of single persons, and it was only after 1891 that the average household size in England and Wales began to decline from about 4.5 persons to about half that level a century later.

Men and women often occupy contrasting residential and living spaces, women having been much confined to the domestic sphere. The practice of purdah in some Muslim and Hindu societies represents the ultimate in gender domestic segregation, drastically restricting the social and economic roles of women, very different from their greater freedom of space and movement in Latin America and Sub-Saharan Africa (Hertrich and Locoh, 1999: 26-7).

Many of these diverse patterns of sex ratios will be examined in more detail in the following chapters, which concern the three main factors influencing variations in sex ratios.

CHAPTER 3

MORE MALE BIRTHS

3.1 Sex Ratios at Birth

The first of the three dynamic factors influencing overall sex ratios is the sex
ratio at birth (sometimes initialised as SRB), particularly the general preponderance of male births over female births. Although that preponderance at country
level is usually only about 104–8 males per 100 female births, the SRB has been
perhaps the most consistent factor affecting sex ratios among large populations,
as it appears to be remarkably constant world-wide. On the other hand, generally the SRB has had less effect on the overall sex ratios of populations than
sex and gender differences in mortality and much less effect on the sex ratios of
small populations than differential migration. This is largely because only 1–4%
of a population may be born in any one year, and male births rarely exceed
female births by more than 10%, whereas sex ratios of deaths are often larger
than those of births and the gender compositions of migration streams are
becoming much more variable.

Nevertheless, sex ratio at birth is naturally important to the reproductivity of
populations, because only females reproduce. It is possible to have an increase in
the birth rate yet a decline in the number of female births. That is why demographers have used *gross reproduction rates* (GRRs) and *net reproduction rates*
(NRRs) to take account of sex ratios, the GRR being the average number of
daughters that would be born to a woman during her lifetime if she passed
through the childbearing ages experiencing the average age-specific fertility
pattern of a given period, and the NRR being more refined in that it also
incorporates the effect of age-specific mortality rates.

The *live birth sex ratio* or *masculinity ratio at birth* is occasionally called the
secondary sex ratio, to distinguish it from the *primary sex ratio* at conception and
the *tertiary sex ratio* at the time of enumeration. The primary sex ratio is generally

accepted to be very much higher than the secondary sex ratio because of higher prenatal male mortality; it has been variously estimated up to 160, but is possibly of the order of 123 to 130 (Bittles *et al.*, 1993). With estimates of between one-third and one-half of all embryos suffering spontaneous abortion, and some mis-carriages taking place so early that they are unrecognised, it should not be sur-prising that the topic is not easily investigated and that estimates of primary sex ratios are only vague. Excess mortality of male foetuses by miscarriage tends to occur throughout the period of gestation, so the male surplus at conception is gradually whittled down to roughly 110 by full term and to about 105 babies born live. Certainly it is a factor of *perinatal mortality*, which is the sum of foetal mortality after 28 weeks of pregnancy and of mortality during the first week of life. Even at birth, male preponderance is further reduced, as there is a high sex ratio of stillborn babies, possibly because male babies are generally larger and subjected to greater trauma at birth. Of course, the sex-differential is not the only differential of perinatal mortality – it is high among premature babies, poorer parents, first-born children, obese mothers, and younger and older mothers.

So on the whole, it is a good long-term bet that most babies are male, but one shouldn't expect to make a lot of money on it, because you need to bet on a lot of babies to achieve any profit! It would usually be a better bet for hospital births, because their sex ratios at birth tend to be higher than normal as male births tend to cause more complications and therefore often take place in hos-pital, at least in more advanced countries.

In most populations the male preponderance at birth has subsequently been reduced by excess male mortality throughout life. Some have said that there are more male births in order to make up for more male deaths, that it is nature's way of ensuring some sort of parity in numbers of the two sexes. But this is difficult to prove, and in any case it does not seem to be working very well. When unaffected by deliberate human action, such as sex-related abortion and infanticide, the variation in SRBs has not been very great, but in recent years the growth in the incidence of sex-selective abortions in a number of countries in East, South East and South Asia appears to have contributed to considerable distortions in SRBs. However, as William James (1997c) suggests, it is im-possible to infer current sex-related infanticide or induced abortion from the present reported birth sex ratios in any particular population, because they are also very dependent on past sex prejudice, which is unquantifiable. As we shall see later in this chapter, the distinct possibility that sex selection at birth will become a common occurrence during the next century has raised even more fears about a great increase in this natural male preponderance at birth, with the possibility of major imbalances in the numbers of male and female babies in some parts of Asia if traditional son preference continues to prevail.

In the great majority of national populations, with very few exceptions in MDCs, the normal preponderance of male births has been in the range of 104–108 per 100 female births (see Table 3.1 and Figure 3.1). As might be

Table 3.1　Recent Recorded Sex Ratios at Birth (SRBs) in Selected Countries

LDCs	Year	SRB	MDCs	Year	SRB
AFRICA			**N. AMERICA**		
Cape Verde	1990	107.8	Canada	1995	105.2
Egypt	1992	109.3	USA	1991	104.6
Mauritius	1995	100.8			
Morocco	1993	104.9	**ASIA & OCEANIA**		
Tunisia	1995	107.3	Japan	1996	105.6
Zimbabwe	1992	101.6	Australia	1996	105.9
			New Zealand	1993	106.5
C. AMERICA					
Cuba	1995	115.3	**EUROPE**		
El Salvador	1992	100.2	Albania	1989	107.1
Guatemala	1993	104.3	Austria	1996	105.3
Mexico	1996	101.8	Belgium	1992	104.9
Panama	1994	104.5	Bosnia-Herzegovina	1991	105.3
Puerto Rico	1996	106.1	Bulgaria	1995	104.7
Trinidad & Tobago	1995	104.5	Croatia	1996	107.7
			Czech Republic	1996	105.5
S. AMERICA			Denmark	1995	105.9
Brazil	1994	104.2	Estonia	1996	105.6
Chile	1996	105.1	Finland	1996	105.3
Ecuador	1996	104.2	France	1994	105.1
Paraguay	1991	105.8	Germany	1996	105.8
Uruguay	1988	103.7	Greece	1995	108
Venezuela	1996	107.5	Hungary	1996	106.1
ASIA			Iceland	1996	105.4
Bahrain	1995	106	Ireland	1996	108.7
Bangladesh	1988	107	Italy	1995	106.4
China	1989	113.9	Latvia	1996	108
Cyprus	1996	107.6	Lithuania	1996	104.8
Hong Kong	1996	106.6	Luxembourg	1996	110.2
Israel	1995	105.5	Netherlands	1996	106.1
North Korea	1993	105	Norway	1996	107
South Korea	1995	113.4	Poland	1996	105.3
Kuwait	1996	105	Portugal	1996	108.3
Malaysia	1996	106.4	Romania	1996	105.7
Pakistan	1993	110	Slovakia	1995	104.7
Philippines	1993	108.7	Slovenia	1996	107
Qatar	1992	107.1	Spain	1995	106.4
Singapore	1997	107.9	Sweden	1996	104.3
Sri Lanka	1995	103.6	Switzerland	1996	105
Thailand	1994	106.2	United Kingdom	1996	105.5
Turkey	1989	106.5	Yugoslavia	1995	108.6

Source of data: UN *Demographic Yearbook 1997* (1999).

expected, SRBs are rather more variable in LDCs. A few Central and South American countries (e.g. Ecuador, El Salvador, Mexico and Uruguay) record lower SRBs of 100–104, but hardly any country in the world records more female births than male births. In contrast, a few Asian countries (e.g. China, Pakistan, Philippines, Singapore, South Korea) and Cuba now report much

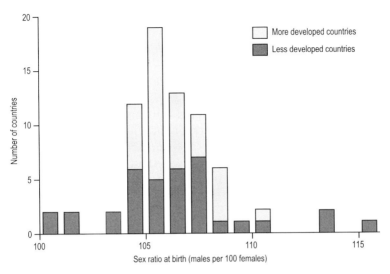

Figure 3.1   Sex ratios at birth of 73 countries in the late twentieth century.

higher than average SRBs of 110 or more, mainly for reasons already briefly mentioned. The median sex ratio at birth in the 1990s for 73 countries listed in the UN *Demographic Yearbook 1997* (1999) was about 106, with a limited range if vital registration is reasonably accurate. Unfortunately, in most countries it is not, and in the poorer LDCs it is frequently so seriously defective that live birth sex ratios based on registered births may not be very meaningful, partly because there is usually better registration of male births.

The level of male preponderance at birth is not unchanging. In England and Wales, the sex ratio at birth is now about 105, rising from 104 in 1911 to 106 in 1951–71, but falling slightly since. Slight declines in the ratio of male to female births have also been recorded in several other industrialised countries: in Denmark and Netherlands during 1950–94 and Canada and the United States during 1970–90, as well as in Sweden, Norway, Finland and Germany (Davis, Gottlieb and Stampnitzky, 1998). It has been suggested that decline in family size might be a factor; nineteenth century German data seemed to indicate the probability that the child is a boy is greater in larger families (Lindsey and Altham, 1998). In contrast, sex ratios at birth in several South European countries (Portugal, Italy, Greece and the former Yugoslavia) are still as high as 107–8.

Sex ratios at birth tend to oscillate, even seasonally; in England, for example, from about 104 in November to 106 in May. Similar slight seasonal variations have been noted in the United States among different populations, with the highest ratios in early summer and the lowest in the fall and winter. A recent analysis of the records of the German Bureau of Statistics from 1946 to 1995 indicated a highly significant though low-amplitude rhythm with two peaks in May and December and two troughs in March and October, but no correlations were found between sex ratios and seasonal birth rates during this period (Lerchl, 1998).

In many MDCs, twentieth century reductions in perinatal mortality have particularly favoured male babies. This largely accounts for the increase, albeit small, in the live birth sex ratios in Britain during much of the twentieth century. So advances in medical care during pregnancy have not only improved the success rates of conception but have also enhanced slightly the chances of male survival. Unfortunately, as we shall see, these advances are used in some LDCs to greatly exaggerate the surplus of male births through sex-selective abortion.

3.2   Why Are There More Male Births?

In the past, people have postulated all manner of biological and behavioural factors causing male or female births, but for most of human history until the last few decades the sex of a newborn child has been seen as a fact of life, about which a couple could do very little. The sex of children was largely viewed as an act of God, to whom one should give thanks. Most couples have felt that there was a 50 : 50 chance of a boy or a girl, but over the centuries a wide variety of techniques were used to try to alter the odds by influencing the sex of their babies. Probably very few of them were useful. Robert Winston (1997: 28) has said that

> "the ancients tended to believe that boys were generated from the right side, girls from the left. Coital position was therefore considered important to influence the humours forming the fetus. Timing of intercourse during the menstrual cycle, delaying orgasm, changing the amount of salt in the diet or the acidity of the vagina, taking up less stressful living, have all at times been favoured methods of influencing the sex of the fetus. There is little evidence for the efficacy of any of these remedies".

It has even been suggested that conceiving under a tree helped to produce a boy, but the effectiveness of this technique has probably never been researched! More surprisingly, Marie Stopes, the famous birth control pioneer, recommended that marital beds be aligned with the earth's magnetic field if a boy was wanted. The suggestions are endless, and have been put forward with differing levels of confidence, seriousness and scientific rationale. It is now realised that the topic is so complex, multi-dimensional and multi-disciplinary that it has defied so far a generally accepted scientific explanation. The difficulty has been in distinguishing between the relative contributions of various factors.

A number of overviews of SRBs have been attempted from different perspectives (e.g. Teitelbaum, 1972; Chahnazarian, 1988; James, 1987a and b). In the early 1970s, the demographer Michael Teitelbaum (1972) reviewed a list of 29 mainly behavioural factors that have been associated with sex ratio at birth (see Table 3.2), including both serious and less serious suggestions. Teitelbaum's analysis suggested that birth order (i.e. the classification of births according to the number of previous births to the mother) seemed to be the most important factor, the masculinity ratio diminishing irregularly from the first birth to the second and so on, although the evidence did not appear to be particularly conclusive. Like many others before him and since, he noted the tendency for the number of male births to rise during recurrent post-war 'baby booms', and suggested that it may well be associated with the rise in the number of first marriages and in the incidence of first births during post-war years rather than the more popular suggestion that it was a natural demographic compensation for the loss of men during wars and later suggestions that it is related to coital rates. It was also noted that as birth rates decline the proportion of first

Table 3.2 Factors Associated with Live-Birth Sex Ratio, According to Teitelbaum (1972)

 1. Birth order
 2. Family size
 3. Sex of first born
 4. Maternal age
 5. Paternal age
 6. Relative ages of father and mother
 7. General genetic factors
 8. Race and colour
 9. Inbreeding and outbreeding
10. Radiation damage
11. Ancestral longevity
12. Physique and temperament
13. Baldness of father
14. Cigarette smoking
15. Coffee drinking
16. Blood groups
17. Birth control
18. Artificial insemination
19. Frequency of intercourse
20. Time of conception during menstrual cycle
21. Seasonal and monthly variation
22. Geographical and climatic conditions
23. Illegitimacy
24. Parental occupation
25. Socio-economic status and conditions
26. War and post-war periods
27. Urban/rural and other differences
28. High speed stresses
29. Sex of last prior pregnancy

Source: Teitelbaum, 1972: 98–9.

births rises and thus the preponderance of male births. In addition, the study indicated "a significantly lower sex ratio for negroes than for whites, and a significant negative association between sex ratio and socio-economic status" (Teitelbaum, 1972: 104). In fact, it is now generally recognised that oriental sex ratios at birth tend to be higher than white birth sex ratios which are higher than those of blacks (James, 1987b).

It has also often been remarked that people of high social status and greater prosperity tend to have more sons than normal. For example, although they are a somewhat limited statistical sample, Presidents of the United States have had 90 sons but only 61 daughters, and studies of 'the great and the good' mentioned in the *Who's Who* of various countries also seem to confirm this phenomenon (Smith, 1997: 88). Going to the other end of the lengthy scale from wealth to poverty, a study of 3282 children born to 684 women in a rural area of the Central African Republic appears to confirm the association between maternal malnutrition and low sex ratio at birth, a finding consistent with animal experiments (Andersson and Bergström, 1998).

Two other study factors, paternal age and maternal age, did not appear in Teitelbaum's study to be associated with the sex ratio, but John Manning and colleagues (1997), studying 301 English and Welsh families with age differences ranging from husbands 15 years older to 9 years younger than their wives, found that women who marry men much older than themselves have a greater chance of having a boy as their first child, and that where the husband is younger or up to 5 years older a daughter is the likeliest first child. Consequently, they suggested that a large age difference between parents tends to predict the sex of the child, but this general finding was not confirmed by Astolfi and Zonta (1999) for children born in Lombardy during 1990 and 1991.

In a later review of the impressively large scientific literature on human sex ratio at birth from the viewpoint of a biologist rather than a demographer, William H. James (1987a) found that birth sex ratio

"varies (if only slightly) with a large number of variables, among which may be mentioned race, season, wartime, legitimacy, birth order and paternal age. In addition one may suspect variation also with the psychological status of parents, the smoking status of the mother, the handedness of parents, the location of an anomolously implanted pregnancy, occupation and maternal age. None of this variation is substantial: however, more recent research stemming from medical (rather than demographic) sources seems to have identified a few conditions with which sex ratio varies substantially, e.g. time of insemination within the cycle, some forms of parental disease at the time of conception, hormonal treatment of the parents for subfertility or other condition, and inadvertent exposure of parents to deleterious chemicals".

It will be seen that some of these (handedness, hormonal treatment, deleterious chemicals) are additional to Teitelbaum's list. He went on to hypothesise (1987b)

> "that hormone levels of both parents at the time of conception affect the probability of a male birth, high levels of oestrogen (*the female hormone*) and testosterone (*the male hormone*) increasing this probability, and high levels of gonadotropin (*formed in the pituitary gland*) decreasing it".

This hypothesis appears to accommodate many of the substantial and slight variations in sex ratio at birth already mentioned.

The fact is that the biological reasons for male preponderance at birth are still somewhat obscure. In essence, the sex of a child is determined by gametes. All eggs have one X chromosome (i.e. gynosperm), while the sperm fertilising the egg may carry either a Y chromosome (i.e. androsperm) producing males, or an X chromosome producing females. Thus a combination of X and X chromosomes in the fertilised egg will produce a female, while an X and a Y will produce a male. Often it is stated that the faster swimming speed and greater agility of Y-bearing sperm, which have a longer tail and a lighter head, accounts for male preponderance at birth, but according to Winston (1997) there has been much rather inconclusive discussion, as for many other aspects of the matter.

Recent research publicised in the media (e.g. *Independent*, 28 June 1999) has suggested that male occupations with significantly increased incidences of defective sperm are associated with reduced numbers of male children. In a study of 969 children, birth sex ratios were established according to fathers' occupation, and these were compared with the incidence of sperm defects in over 1400 infertile couples. It was found that men who were office-based had less defective sperm and higher SRBs than men such as motor mechanics who were exposed to toxins and noxious chemicals. City dwellers affected by urban pollution are particularly prone to low sperm counts.

Considerable discussion and controversy have ranged around the significance of high coital rates to high sex ratios at birth. It is often stated that when coital rates are frequent, as during the early stages of married life, an egg is more likely to meet fresh Y-bearing sperm and thus the sex ratio at birth is higher than later in marriage. J.F. Martin (1994) suggested that

> "sex ratios at birth may vary with birth order in a conjugal union, maternal age, form of marriage, and political relations between the sexes. The behavioural variable which appears to tie all these factors to sex ratio at birth is coital frequency",

although the bases of this connection are uncertain. Valerie J. Grant (1995) challenged this hypothesis and proposed an alternative one based on biological dominance resting on the possibility of differential sperm access under the control of the female. Martin (1995) found the timing of insemination relative to ovulation and the frequency of insemination inadequate explanations of the sex ratio at birth, and proposed "a new synthetic model of sex determination in which the sex of the offspring is powerfully determined by the state of the cervical mucus" which was "shown to be a function of hormonal factors endogenous to the female in interaction with the effects of previous inseminations".

W.H. James (1997a) has suggested that while coital rates and cervical mucus may play a part in sex ratios at birth, hormones may well have a decisive influence. Both testosterone and oestrogen encourage the conception of boys, while gonadotropins encourage the conception of girls either by affecting the cervical mucus or by restraining the Y-bearing sperm. Perhaps supporting this hormone theory is the proposition that dominant women with high testosterone levels (e.g. barristers, managers) appear to produce more boys than less dominant women (e.g. beauty contestants, clerical workers). Does this mean that as women move into previously male-dominated occupations and have higher testosterone levels, the sex ratio at birth will rise? James has affirmed that the correlation between coital rates and sex ratio is secondary to correlations of both with time of fertilisation, that parental hormone levels at conception are causally associated with sex ratios at birth, and that they answer the persistent question concerning the stability of the human sex ratio at birth. He has declared (1995) that it

"is stabilised only to a minor extent by the direct processes of natural selection. Instead, the major factors stabilising sex ratio seem to be behavioural (coital rates) and psychological (parental perceptions of adult sex ratios). It is suggested that parental hormone levels are (a) a consequence of perceived adult sex ratios, and (b) a cause of sex ratio in the next generation, thus providing the basis for a negative feedback process stabilising the sex ratio".

In this discussion about the biology of sex ratios, Nancy S. Coney and Wade C. Mackey (1996) have suggested that

"the dynamics of the human sex ratio has two interpretations. One interpretation is that the sperm essentially operate independently of each other, and gender determination at conception is approximated by coin-flip analogy. This interpretation forms the basis of Weinberg's Rule. The second interpretation is that the woman's ecological situation biases her toward/ away from androsperm or gynosperm, i.e. sperm do not operate independently of each other at conception (or differential mortality occurs as a function of gender during gestation). This interpretation forms the basis of the notion that the human sex ratio is facultative ... (i.e. *able to exist under more than one set of conditions*). Data have been gathered by adherents to support both interpretations. The conundrum of potentially mutually exclusive explanations being simultaneously accepted is examined by the authors".

But W.H. James (1997b) has argued that the number of mechanisms underlying variations in sex ratio at birth (e.g. steroid hormone levels) is much smaller than the number of variables by which it varies, and he suggests that the underlying mechanisms should be studied to see if they operate in conformity with facultative theory.

So far there does not appear to be any absolutely clear-cut answer to the question why biologically populations tend to have a preponderance of male births. Biologists are getting closer to the truth, but it seems that the answer will be multi-dimensional, and one in which macro-generalisations result from micro-diversity.

3.3   The Persistence of Son Preference

The high incidence of male births is linked in many parts of the world with the prevalence of son preference. The desire for sons and the belief that boys matter more than girls is an attitude which has long been present in most countries. It is particularly prevalent in those societies where sons are the main source of economic security for parents in their old age, especially where women have little economic independence, and it is most deeply entrenched in many more traditional cultures with patriarchal social structures. Son preference is not easily overcome, because it is linked more to cultural and religious values than to levels of economic development. It is, for example, especially common in cultures with *patrilocal marriage* traditions (where brides move to live with their husband's family and are therefore largely lost to their own family). So naturally the strength of son preference varies greatly from society to society, from country to country and from time to time, and has never been under more general attack than now (Ross, 1982: 669).

It must be stressed that son preference is not confined to parental choice of the sex of a future child, but is expressed to a variable degree as male preference and as female neglect throughout childhood and adulthood. As will be seen in Chapter 4, both are unfortunately very marked in some cultures, notably in many different Asian countries such as Bangladesh, China, India, Jordan, Nepal, Pakistan, South Korea and Syria, to the great disadvantage of women in general and with considerable impact upon their morbidity and mortality rates at all ages. In recent decades, the significance of this form of sex discrimination has changed dramatically and worryingly in connection with SRBs, as new methods have become available to couples to directly influence the sex of their babies.

Son preference has long been widespread in mainly agricultural rural societies, and is particularly evident today in those LDCs where rural populations still prevail, as for example in much of East, South East, South and South West Asia as well as in much of Africa and Latin America. There, sons are usually seen as more economically productive than daughters, even at a young age, and are also regarded as providers of old-age security for ageing parents, as carriers of the family name, as performers of ancestral rites and as heirs to the family property. They are therefore valued for their long-term benefits. In some societies, as for example those with a Confucian tradition, the family is seen to be dying if there are no sons, an attitude reinforced by the *yin* and *yang* philosophy of nature, whereby the *yang* (positive, bright and male) principle always dominated the *yin* (negative, dark and female). It is sad to reflect that in so many societies in the past, sons have been regarded as an asset, daughters as a liability. This materialistic view was based on an attitude that the economic value of the labour and help of daughters was lost when they married and left home, a view that was intensified in those societies where daughters have required an expensive dowry on marriage, where marriage has been exogamous, and where daughters have not normally contributed thereafter to the upkeep of their parents.

Son preference is not universal, and in many countries parents want at least one daughter as well as sons. There is also evidence of a slight preference for daughters in Venezuela and Jamaica, and among some ethnic groups in Zambia, Cambodia and the Philippines, although it is normally more benign than son preference because it does not imperil the welfare of boys (Seager, 1997; Hill and Ball, 1999). Strickland and Tuffrey (1997) also report on female-biased sex ratios at birth among high social status Nepalese, where women's work is an important factor. They link it with parental investment theory, which postulates that where physical condition varies significantly SRBs will be correlated with social status. A somewhat different case is that of the people of Chiang Mai province in northern Thailand, where daughters are expected to support parents and younger siblings and unfortunately often do so through their activities as prostitutes within the extensive and notorious sex industry of that country (Jones and Pardthaisong, 1998).

In general, the strength and prevalence of son preference only diminishes with a marked rise in the status of women. It has diminished most significantly in Western societies, particularly during the last two centuries when industrialisation and urbanisation have meant the migration of many millions of men and women to work in the cities. These massive socio-economic changes were accompanied by reversals in the inter-generational flows of wealth; children provided less economically to families living in the cities than they did in rural areas and they cost more to keep, so the advantage of and preference for a son was greatly reduced. It has not declined to the extent of being replaced by strong daughter preference, although those days may come sooner than expected with the socio-economic changes occurring in recent decades, particularly the rise in service and light manufacturing industries, leading to a decline in demand for male labour and a growing demand for female labour. Girls are not only beginning to excel over boys at school and in getting a job, they are seen to be easier to raise and to employ, and are less likely to get into trouble or be involved in crime. Certainly, many city-dwelling couples in advanced countries prefer daughters, though many are happier to express no preference at all.

A recent review of the literature over the past 45 years concerning men and women's separate choices for an only child in MDCs, mostly in North America, has revealed clear differences in preference between the two sexes (Marleau and Maheu, 1998). Consistently, at least 70% of men have preferred a son to a daughter. Among women, on the other hand, preferences were more complicated: previous studies indicated that while non-pregnant women tended to prefer a son to a daughter, women pregnant for the first time tended to prefer a daughter to a son, but a high proportion expressed no preference at all, possibly because they hesitated to reveal a preference or wished to conceal it (not least from a partner). The most recent studies seem to indicate a growing preference among women for a daughter, especially among educated women, obviously a matter of considerable significance in countries where one-child families are increasingly common. These preferences for boys and girls vary from country to country among different socio-economic, religious and age groups as well as over time, so there are evident social implications not least for the success or otherwise of marriages and partnerships. Obviously, this is a changing area of research where there is still much work to be done (Marleau and Maheu, 1998).

In contrast with most MDCs, son preference still prevails in oriental societies and most of the developing world, despite its declining strength in recent decades following improvements in the status of women, involving delays in their marriage as well as increases in their education and their employment in the labour force. Women in East and South East Asian countries and many Latin American countries are now contributing greatly to modern economic growth, and this is engendering changing attitudes towards son preference. Of course, women are still a very long way from anything like equal status, as cultures do not change overnight, but there are clear signs of a transformation in social attitudes.

It has often been argued that high fertility is partly caused by couples who would like to have a surviving son and go on reproducing until they have one or two boys or perhaps a child of each sex. In order to emphasise this point, Christian Seidl (1995) even entitled a paper "The desire for a son is the father of many daughters: a sex ratio paradox". However, evidence is far from clear that high fertility will persist as long as there is strong son preference, because in some countries where son preference is still strong there has been rapid fertility decline. For example, amongst the Chinese in Malaysia, whose son preference is greater than that of Malays and Indians, it does not seem to be a constraint upon fertility decline (Pong, 1994). Similarly, in South Korea, total fertility rates declined between 1960 and 1990 from 6.0 to 1.6 despite strong preference for male offspring. Women with one son are less likely to have another child and take longer to conceive it (Larsen *et al.*, 1998). As long ago as 1985, Fred Arnold remarked that generally in high-fertility societies son preference may not have a very great effect on fertility because there couples choose to have a lot of children no matter whether they are sons or daughters. Moreover, in low-fertility societies couples tend to have few children irrespective of their sex. In theory, the effect of son preference should be greatest where the transition from high to low fertility is under way, which is a characteristic feature of very many LDCs nowadays.

> Studies by Fred Arnold (1986) in *Egypt* showed that son preference did not have as much impact on overall fertility levels as was previously thought. He found that couples increased their use of modern contraceptives in direct proportion to an increase in the number of sons. Couples with all sons were 2–6 times more likely to use modern contraception than were couples with all daughters. There were also fewer all-daughter families than one would expect. But this son preference was seen to be unlikely to have a great effect on Egypt's fertility, as only a small proportion of couples found themselves faced with a decision to have another child merely because they had not yet had a son. By biological chance, more than one couple in two will have a son first, and a son second, and so on, and consequently the great majority of all couples will have at least one son early in their childbearing lives. Arnold was able to show that son preference has relatively little impact on family planning behaviour of couples.

Extending his study to 27 LDCs, Arnold found that if there were no son preference at all, contraceptive use would increase by less than 3.7%. The effect of son preference on contraceptive use was strongest in Asia, where in many countries fertility had fallen rapidly in any case. In Africa, he estimated that the total elimination of son preference would make only about 2.9% difference in contraceptive use.

Son preference appears to have had a striking effect on sex ratios at birth in some Asian countries, notably China, Taiwan and South Korea. As we shall see, it seems that through the advent of female abortions coinciding with fertility decline, there has been an acceleration of sex discrimination at birth (Gu and Roy, 1995).

> In *India*, during 1981–91 there were 112 boys born for every 100 girls, compared with the normal average of 106 during the earlier period 1949–58, a fact which seems to be associated with son preference. The 1992–93 National Family Health Survey (NFHS) of India enabled analysis of the

incidence of son preference and its impact on fertility decline in 19 Indian states. "When asked to describe their ideal family composition, Indian women as a whole said they wanted 50% more sons than daughters. Women in every state wanted more sons, but the preference for sons was particularly strong in Punjab, Rajasthan, Uttar Pradesh, Bihar and Gujarat. It was weakest in Kerala, Delhi, Assam, Goa, Karnataka and Tamil Nadu" (Arnold, Choe and Roy, 1996). A second method of measuring son preference was based on women's stated intention to stop having children, those with sons being more likely to stop than those with daughters. By this measure, son preference was strongest in Haryana and Rajasthan and weakest in Kerala. A third measure, based on contraceptive use, showed that women in every state were more likely to practise family planning if they had two sons rather than two daughters. By this measure, Rajasthan had particularly strong son preference, and it was relatively weak in Kerala, Andhra Pradesh, Goa and Tamil Nadu. So by all three measures, son preference was strongest in the northern and central regions of India (except the capital, Delhi) and weakest in the south, a reflection of profound cultural contrasts. Other indicators, such as sex discrimination in the care of children, support this finding and generally son preference tends to be strong where fertility is high, although inevitably in a culturally complex country like India there are exceptions.

Son preference has been seen in India to have counteracted the Indian government's aim to reduce fertility, because couples may not stop having children after having achieved their desired family size if they have not reached their desired number of sons. The NFHS survey suggested that national fertility would be reduced by 8% in the absence of son preference, and that an effort to reduce son preference would have considerable benefits in reducing fertility and therefore population growth. It is recognised, however, that changing the attitudes of couples towards son preference in India is not an easy problem to overcome. It is not attained merely by increasing female education. Although literate Indian women have less children than illiterate women, and are better equipped to have less children, literacy does not necessarily change their attitude to having sons. Similarly, although urban women have less children than rural women, they show similar or even stronger effects of son preference on fertility levels. Consequently, community programmes for the social development of women must clearly be adapted to local cultural traditions.

In *China*, historical records show that son preference has always been present. Associated with deep-rooted Confucian traditions, patriarchal attitudes and sex discrimination, it has led to a considerable shortage of girls. Son preference and girl shortage have been highlighted in recent decades by the Chinese government's introduction of the drastic one-child policy in 1979 and its spread during the 1980s. Writing at the time, Fred

Arnold and Liu Zhaoxiang (1986: 243) remarked that son preference was evidenced by a variety of measures:

- couples with one daughter were less likely to have obtained a one-child certificate than couples with one son;
- after receiving the certificate they were more likely to violate its provisions by having a second child;
- couples without a son were less likely to use contraception than couples with a son;
- pregnant women without a son were less likely to have an abortion than those with at least one son; and
- sex ratios of children were progressively smaller among couples with more children.

The one-child policy was most effective in urban centres, but rural areas were not able to sustain it so well because peasants wanted sons, and therefore the government subsequently moved to a slightly more relaxed 'one son or two child' policy, the second child being permitted if the first child was a girl. Unfortunately, the outcome of this policy was to institutionalise son preference as state policy, and it is reflected in the problem of millions of 'missing girls and women' (see section 1.1).

The persistence of son preference in China is indicated in the recent striking rise in its SRBs, the variations of which among Chinese provinces have been shown to be closely related to variations in the degree of son preference (Poston *et al.*, 1997). The number of boys born per 100 girls in China was usually around 106, but rose to about 112 in 1986 and then to about 114–116 during 1989–93. A profound shortage of baby girls was soon recognised. Whereas in 1990 there were 110 boys aged 0–4 years per 100 girls, by 1995 the sample census showed that this ratio had risen to 118:100. Subsequently, rising SRBs were accepted as a reality and became a matter of considerable concern, expressed partly with reference to a number of consequential problems such as 'the imbalance in the first marriage market' and 'the burden of elderly people without male offspring' (Li, Tuljapurkar and Feldman, 1995). It has been estimated that from the year 2010 there will be a surplus of about one million males per year in the first marriage market, and that this will pose considerable social and cultural challenges. The imbalance in the numbers of potential bridegrooms and brides has even been seen as a reason for the rising tide of prostitution in China, but obviously many other factors are involved. The main causes of the excess of male births have been variously identified – under-reporting of female births, female infanticide, adoption-out of female children and female abortions – causes which in the absence of hard data have been given different weightings (Zeng *et al.*, 1993), and which will be examined shortly.

Although the long tradition of son preference has abated to some extent in the cities of China, especially among more educated couples, it is still commonplace in rural areas, where young married women often live in dread that their first child will be a girl. The Chinese press has contained many cases of women being beaten by their husbands or by other members of the family for not having produced the desired son. In many rural areas couples are now allowed to have a second child without penalties, as long as there is a gap of five years between the first and second child and they are planned under the quota system. Rural families who obey the family planning rules, which are integrated with rural development proposals, tend to be given priority in getting loans, materials and technical assistance from the local government. Obviously, poorer families who have too many children are further disadvantaged. Some couples go so far as to conceal the birth of a girl, who may be sent to distant relatives so that they can try again for a boy.

The problem of 'missing girls' is most serious in the traditional Han regions of eastern China, the densely populated half of China where the one-child family policy has been implemented most. In the vast and more open spaces of western China where ethnic minorities are more common, women with no sons or several daughters have been likely to continue to try to achieve a son even at ages and parities when they would normally have stopped childbearing (Anderson and Silver, 1995). On the other hand, Barbara Anderson and Brian Silver found disproportionately feminine sex ratios at birth for couples who had several sons and no daughters, suggesting that there is a preference for girls under certain conditions, and that whereas much of the discussion about sex preference has been concerned with sex-differential mortality, it ought to focus more on sex-selective infanticide, abortion and adoption.

3.4 Female Infanticide, Abandonment and Adoption

A tradition of infanticide has been common in many societies around the world, whereby unwanted, illegitimate, deformed and even twin babies have been killed or abandoned to die. Infanticide was long practised in many ancient cultures, including those of Greece, Rome and China, but has continued more recently among various hunter-gatherer peoples of Africa and Asia, as well as for example among Inuit, New Guineans and Polynesians (Hill and Ball, 1999). In the hostile or difficult physical environments where most such peoples live, it has been mainly practised to increase the survival of other children or because the mother is a teenager where there are taboos about early sexual relationships (Hausfater and Hrdy, 1984). However, infanticide is not confined to traditional societies. In more modern societies where marriage break-ups and remarriage are common, there is a well known but fortunately rare tendency by some stepfathers to commit homicide or infanticide of their stepchildren; apparently in North America it is sixty times more likely by stepfathers than by biological fathers.

Infanticide has been used largely as a method of postnatal sex selection, and as parents invest differentially in newborn boys and girls female infanticide has undoubtedly greatly exceeded male infanticide (Langer, 1974). The killing of girl babies was frequent in many hunter-gatherer and agricultural societies, especially in those patriarchal societies involved in warfare (Bandarage, 1997: 120–2). Few parts of the world have escaped this practice, but it has been more likely to occur where girls are not seen to contribute as much as boys to the household income or where poor families are expected to provide large dowries for them (Hill and Ball, 1999). It has been long-standing among some high-caste communities in north-west India and also in western China, and in both regions it still occurs to some extent.

In north-west *India* it has resulted mainly from the problems of arranging suitable marriages for daughters and from the high cost of dowries. Analysing the 1872 census in the western region of United Provinces, Miller (1981: 65) concluded that "one-fourth of the population ... murdered one-half of their female offspring", although efforts by the British to suppress the practice led to the Infanticide Act of 1870 and a subsequent decline. Of course, the conditions are now very different, partly because it is condemned by law and religion in India, but its occurrence in recent years has been affected by the increasing diffusion of the small family norm and the desire for a son. Numbers are naturally vague, but it has been estimated that as many as 10,000 baby girls are killed each year in India (Neft and Levine, 1997: 307).

In *China*, female infanticide has apparently experienced a resurgence despite state discouragement, partly because of the profound social pressures exerted by the harshness of the one-child family programme during the 1980s and the prevalence of son preference. Terence Hull (1990) reported that the infants killed at birth were overwhelmingly female. Inevitably, accurate data are not available, and some argue that female infanticide cannot be widely practised because in a society like that of China all the neighbours would know about it, while others have suggested that there is considerable scope for such a practice in a society where births are only recognised when the baby has survived for a month and where much perinatal mortality thus goes unreported.

The social pressures of restrictive birth planning policies in China are also reflected in a revival of the practices of baby girls being given away for adoption without registering their births, and of the neglect and abandonment of girls, practices which are seen to be closely linked and which particularly affect high parity daughters in families without sons (Johnson *et al.*, 1998). Undoubtedly, many of these girls have subsequently died and others have been the reason for the excessive number of abandoned girls in state-run orphanages, whose grave human rights abuses and the exceptionally high death rates among their inmates have been the subject of numerous objections from other countries, notably the United States. Campaigners against the one-child policy have stated that about a million baby girls are abandoned each year, and Human Rights Watch/Asia (1996) have asserted that most of the missing abandoned children die. It has been estimated that in the early 1990s, when conditions were very difficult, up to a half of the children brought into orphanages died, usually within the first few months, but the situation has improved since then, not only through greater state intervention but also through extensive charitable support and international adoptions, especially to the United States and Canada. Fortunately, in the late 1990s there were clear signs that China was intending to revise its adoption law, improving the lot of foundlings and over-worked child welfare centres.

Once again the numbers of adoptions and abandonments of girls in China are not easily estimated, because of so many uncertainties about the numbers dying within or without the welfare system. Some of the children outside of it fare better than those within. As the relative importance of these factors is so uncertain, it is difficult to confirm Asoka Bandarage's (1997: 101) comment that "in China the abandonment and concealing of girls may be more important than sex-selective abortions or infanticide". On the other hand, another assertion that "some parents bring up their daughter surreptitiously to avoid the harsh penalties of the one-child law, even after the relaxation of the one-child policy for rural couples in 1988" is undoubtedly true. These unauthorised girls have grown up as second class citizens receiving few of the benefits accorded to other children, and they are often known as 'black babies'. After examining the 1988 two-per thousand fertility survey of China, Sten Johansson and Ola Nygren (1991) argued that adoption-out of baby girls might account for up to half of the 500,000 'missing girls' per year in the 1980s, and that excess female infant mortality was about 39,000 per year, or about 4 infant deaths per thousand live-born girls. Later authors, including Ansley Coale and Judith Banister (1994), felt that adoption is an inadequate explanation because adopted-in children would be enumerated at the place of destination. However, adopted children are generally under-reported, and a survey by Johnson *et al.* (1998) revealed that there is an evident desire to adopt daughters and a willingness to adopt unrelated children, despite government regulations discriminating against adoptions. So there is no doubt that adoption does account for some of the missing females, as does abandonment.

3.5   The Recent Surge in Sex-Selective Abortions

Sex-selective abortions, essentially female abortions, are now much more common than infanticide. Sadly, sex-selective induced abortions have recently increased throughout the world since the 1970s as a result of the rapid spread of the modern technology that enables prenatal sex testing and the sex pre-determination of unborn foetuses. Three techniques of sex predetermination are now widely available in very many countries:

(1) chorionic villus sampling;
(2) amniocentesis; and
(3) ultrasound.

First available in the West, they were devised for diagnosing genetic disorders, but they are now being increasingly used (abused is perhaps a more appropriate term) in many LDCs for sex predetermination and subsequently for sex-selective abortion. Of the three techniques, the safest, cheapest and most frequently used in developing countries is ultrasound, but as in the case of amniocentesis, it is not accurate until the second trimester of pregnancy. It therefore leads to late abortions with greater physical risks for mothers and profound psychological effects, as well as much less public acceptability. Formerly found only in the more developed countries of the West, ultrasound machines are now mass-produced in East and South Asian countries such as China, India and South Korea and they are extensively used, with increasing demographic repercussions.

Deep-rooted son preference, the widespread occurrence of abortion as a means of family limitation, and the recent introduction of the technology of sex determination have led to a surge in sex-selective abortions. Reliable statistics are not available, but large numbers of these abortions have taken place especially in many populous Asian countries, notably China, South Korea, Taiwan, Malaysia, Indonesia and India, where patriarchal societies prevail and where there is strong pressure for fertility reduction. Gu Baochang and Krishna Roy (1995) found that high sex ratios at birth in East Asian countries are associated with a combination of rapidly falling fertility, continuing son preference and the availability of sex-predetermination techniques, and thus are a negative result of strongly promoted state family planning programmes. Apart from serious psychological and physiological impact upon parents, the situation poses severe ethical and social problems for policy makers (Bandarage, 1997; Park and Cho, 1995). However, in the context of overall fertility reduction it is estimated that sex-selective abortion has only a moderate overall effect.

In **South Korea**, a distorted sex ratio at birth is a new phenomenon (Suh, 1995). In 1993 the SRB averaged 116, with significant regional differences, the higher levels being associated with stronger preference for sons, sex predetermination and sex-selective abortions. The 1990 census indicated that nearly 80,000 female fetuses had been aborted for sex selection during 1986–90, equivalent to about 5% of all female births. Sex predetermination was made illegal in 1987, and the regulations were later strengthened in 1990 and 1994, but the imposition of severe penalties inevitably led to more clandestine activities. Indeed, there appears to have been a rise in the sex ratio of first births, to 118 in 1991, and a decline in the sex ratio of second births, to 104 for second births after a daughter and to 94 for second births after a son. The current ideal family of many South Koreans now appears to be a son followed by a daughter, and they are using sex-selective abortion to achieve their aims.

In **China**, the strong family planning programme over recent decades has undoubtedly played a part in the incidence of sex predetermination. Although sex-selective abortion was forbidden in 1989 and became illegal in 1995, it is said to be still practised widely not only in cities but also in rural areas. Ultra-sound scanners capable of sex detection were introduced in 1982, and by 1992 they were widely available in hospitals even in backward areas. Statistics on the sex of aborted fetuses are of course not readily available, and are unlikely to be reported. Terence Hull (1990) estimated that while induced abortions accounted for 31% of all births in 1978, by 1986 they had risen to 53%, indicating "that increasing numbers of women have been resorting to pregnancy termination to achieve family size targets", and a majority of the abortions are of females. Of course, the government is worried. There are no financial incentives for families who keep their unwanted female babies, but intensive government publicity campaigns focus on the fact that a baby girl is just as much a blessing as a baby boy, for there has been a growing realisation that a rising sex ratio at birth poses a variety of consequential social and demographic problems such as a shortage of potential wives and daughters to care for ageing parents. One consequence of the persistently high SRBs in China and more average SRBs in North Korea is that now many North Korean girls are reported to be travelling to China with a view to marriage. On the other hand, the future may not be so bleak; the evidence of the 1990s suggests that the lower SRBs now found in the more developed cities of Beijing and Shanghai may be a sign for the future.

The effects of sex-selective abortions on the number of 'missing girls' in South Korea and China are to some extent reflected in the SRBs by birth order, although these also reflect female infanticide, adopting-out of girls and perhaps some under-reporting of female births. Demographers argue about the relative importance of these various explanations, but there can be no certainty in such vast populations (Riley and Gardner, 1997: 46–50). During the 1980s, the sex ratios at birth rose sharply for third and later children born in these countries, as revealed by Chai Bin Park and Nam Hoo Cho (1995) and by surveys in China (see Table 3.3). The most remarkable feature of Table 3.3 is the very high sex ratios for late order births in South Korea, although of course those births were relatively few in number.

In **India**, sex-selective abortion is also commonplace, among rich as well

Table 3.3   Reported Sex Ratios at Birth by Birth Order, South Korea and China, 1982 and 1989

Year	Country	1st	2nd	3rd	4th	5th	All births
1982	South Korea	105.5	106.1	109.3	114.2		106.9
	China	106.5	107.2	113.1	115.5	109.5	107.8
1989	South Korea	104.3	112.6	185	208.6		112.1
	China	104.9	120.4	124.6	132.7	129.7	113.8

Source: Asia-Pacific Population Policy, May–June 1995, No. 34, p. 3.

as poor women, and although sex predetermination was banned in government hospitals in 1983 some feel that there is a danger of it becoming a surrogate for female infanticide. Views about it are varied. It has been excused by some as an effective method of population control, and by others as a long-term method of raising the status of women in society through creating a female shortage. In a recent UNICEF report, it was shockingly revealed that of 8000 abortions carried out after amniocentesis at one Bombay hospital all but one of the fetuses were female. Persistent agitation by feminist groups and growing governmental alarm about the drop in its female population – the press publicise an estimated 40 million 'missing women and girls' in India, a figure which it is difficult to confirm or deny – has now led to the Indian government outlawing sex-predetermination tests. Unfortunately, it is reported that corruption ensures that they continue largely unabated (Bandarage, 1997: 100). To counter this process, on 2 October 1997, the anniversary of Mahatma Ghandi's birthday, the government also launched a scheme by which families earning less than 11,000 rupees (ca. £190) per annum who produce a daughter would receive a payment of 550 rupees (ca. under £9) and would be given incentives to encourage them to send their daughters to school. It is hoped that these measures will have a beneficial effect, but unfortunately the evidence suggests that as son preference occurs among both rich and poor in India their impact may not be very great.

In general, enormous ethical, religious and demographic issues are raised by the new technologies which enable sex-selective abortions and their diffusion around the world. They are particularly disturbing because the practice involves the medical profession and results from medical advances. Sex-selective abortions are generally deplored as discriminatory, and governments are asked to legislate against the practice. Goodkind (1996), however, has emphasised the need to consider the relative evils of prenatal and postnatal discrimination, most observers having neglected to balance female abortions against female infanticide. He has argued that daughters carried to term are more likely to be wanted and thus their excess mortality reduced. He has also suggested (1999) that government restrictions on the practice may interfere with the reproductive freedoms and maternal empowerment envisaged by the 1994 Cairo Conference, and may lead to similar demands among other disadvantaged groups (e.g. the congenitally disabled) and to further restrictions on abortion. Whilst stressing that sex-selective abortion is wrong, he suggests that governments should make greater efforts to dilute the pervasive son preference that underlies it.

Attitudes towards these issues obviously differ among the major cultural realms, so their implications are also diverse – much greater in those parts of the world where abortions still occur in their millions as a means of family limitation than in those other parts where they are proscribed or rare. Sex-selective abortions still account for only a small proportion of the extremely high total number of abortions world-wide, estimated by Population Action International to be as many as about 50 million annually (Neft and Levine, 1997: 121–7). Some 38% of the world's population live in countries where abortion is available on request, 46% in countries where it is available in certain conditions (e.g. rape, incest, mother's mental health, impairment of the fetus) and only 16% in countries, mostly Catholic or Islamic, where abortion is legal only to save the mother's life. Even more worrying is that perhaps about 20 million abortions, or 40% of the world total, are illegal, and certainly these often result in more medical complications leading to high maternal mortality and morbidity (see section 4.6).

It is said that abortions will only disappear when contraception is totally effective. Given that the sexual act is said by WHO to take place as often as 42 billion times a year (and presumably this estimate rises with the growth of population), total effectiveness is difficult to imagine, especially when so many conceptions occur unexpectedly. Some form of sex-selective contraception would also have to be devised in order to overcome the unfortunate need felt for sex-selective abortions. At present, that seems a long way off, but surely the twenty-first century will bring such a technical advance.

3.6   The Spectre of Pre-implantation Sex Selection or Gender Choice

The ethical, religious and demographic problems of sex selection will be further exacerbated if recent scientific research brings to fruition the possibility of inter-fering still more with the natural balance of sex ratios at birth. Research has already enabled the separation of X- and Y-bearing sperm, and thus has brought about the possibility of accurate sex selection, or as it is increasingly termed 'gender choice'. At the moment the technology "generally involves passing sperm through a fluid of relatively high density, and/or spinning samples in a centrifuge to isolate those of a particular weight" (Winston, 1997: 29), and subsequently involves *in vitro* fertilisation (IVF). It seems that early in the twenty-first century there will be a very reliable way of sex selection which will merely involve artificial insemination rather than the complexities of IVF and embryo biopsy. Already it seems quite likely that the technique will soon be used in Britain in the reproduction of cattle, in order to increase the number of females and reduce the number of males and thus avoid the annual slaughter of about 600,000 young bull calves. Horse breeders will also be interested, as male foals make better showjumpers and female foals better polo ponies, and pig farmers will also undoubtedly want to produce more sows.

Winston (1997) pointed out that human sex selection is preferable to infanticide and could in fact lead to a rise in the value of the female sex. He also recognised that this new technology would cause a huge ethical debate, the first signs of which are the concerns over pre-implantation genetic diagnosis (PGD), in which embryos are selected to be free of genetic defects prior to implantation in the womb. In comparison with the massive ethical implications arising from any future extension of this process for social, non-medical reasons (e.g. hair or eye colour) in order to produce 'perfect babies', sex selection is only an early stage, but nevertheless it is a matter of real concern, especially in regard to controls.

In **Britain**, the matter is under much stricter control than for example in the United States (where PGD is left to the ethics of the doctor), there being only four clinics licensed for sex selection by the Human Fertilisation and Embryology Authority (HFEA), and this is only allowed for families with a history of gender-linked disease, such as Duchenne muscular dystrophy that affects only males. It is not allowed for merely social reasons. A member of the Authority has been quoted as saying "Children should be valued for themselves and not for their sex. We do not believe that children are commodities that can be selected as if from a supermarket shelf" (*Independent*, 3 July, 1998). That is a view which will find general favour with many of those for whom sex selection smacks of 'designer babies' and 'playing God', particularly when it is merely a matter of couples choosing the sex of their next child in order to 'balance their families'. Certainly a survey carried out by the HFEA a few years ago revealed that the great majority of British people did not want to select the sex of their children. But attitudes change and are different in other cultures and countries, notably in America, so it is questionable whether that view will persist under the pressure of technological advances.

The significance of this ever-changing technology in sex selection is hitting the headlines sooner than expected. Newspapers in 1998 reported that eight British couples who wanted to choose the sex of their babies had already been sent by one Essex fertility clinic to Italy and Saudi Arabia for sex-selection treatment (*Independent*, 3 July 1998), and that others were sent to an American Genetics and IVF Institute in Fairfax, Virginia which allows sex selection for social rather than medical reasons and claims 85% success with selection of girls and 65% with boys (*Independent*, 19

September 1998). There are now dozens of licensed gender clinics of this sort operating in the United States, some of which are offering 'intelligent eggs' from top students of Ivy League colleges. The technique involves detecting the differences in the quantity of DNA in the X- and Y-bearing sperm which have been stained by a fluorescent dye, separating them by laser and injecting them into eggs removed from the ovaries of the woman. After a few days the sexes of the embryos are checked for sex selection. An organiser of the British clinic is quoted as saying "I would like to see the regulations changed. We are doing surrogacy and allowing insemination of lesbians and homosexuals. These are far bigger minefields than sex selection. At the end of the day it is going to come down to couples voting with their feet". And certainly without international legislation, some potential parents will vote accordingly and travel to wherever they can achieve their aims. Even if legislation is passed in individual countries to try to control the diffusion of sex selection, it is extremely doubtful that it could be adequately implemented nationally, and still less could it be adequately enforced on an international scale. There is too much global mobility of people and goods and too few national and international checks for effective control over strong-minded couples seeking to choose the sex of their children. The pressure will certainly grow; early in 2000, the HFEA received an application to choose the sex of their next child from a Tayside couple who were both aged 42 and who had four sons but whose only daughter had died in a tragic bonfire accident.

Some experts in sex selection are perhaps rather more sanguine than most social scientists about the massive social and psychological implications arising from their work. From the demographic viewpoint alone, considerable long-term numerical changes could take place in the balance of sex ratios affecting the whole future of the human species. Micro-demographic decisions by couples about the sex of their children are unlikely to lead to the sort of macro-demographic balances that so far have been broadly achieved naturally. Existing sex imbalances might be further intensified in many parts of the world.

The future of sex selection lies with the increasing rapidity of scientific advances and of their diffusion, as well as their diverse acceptability among different cultures. In many Asian and Muslim countries, where son preference and the practice of female infanticide, abandonment, adoption and abortion have been more or less commonplace, sophisticated new technologies are increasingly available through local manufacture and it is likely that the new technologies of sex selection would be readily and widely adopted by those who could afford them, leading to a growing surplus of male births. The opposite might occur in many developed countries where female roles are increasing more or less continuously, and where sex selection at birth might lead to further growth in the numerical preponderance of females.

Consider one possible but unlikely future scenario, which many men might find appalling but which many women would consider to be a logical progression of present socio-economic trends in those more developed countries where the roles of women are increasing and those of men are either diminishing or being devalued. The scenario is that at an early age men might wish to be rendered infertile by vasectomy after their sperm had been removed and stored in liquid nitrogen, so that samples might be extracted later for artificial insemination of their partners in order to effect a pregnancy (Smith, 1997: 226–7). In these circumstances current methods of contraception would become unnecessary, and male infertility would become the norm. This could be seen as a more or less logical extension of the present frequency of one-parent families in many MDCs, as well as a reflection of the increasing inadequacy of men in modern society and the greater ability of women in adapting to deindustrialisation and the growth of service economies. With gender no longer so strong a predeterminant of social and economic roles, men as reproducers would become redundant in large numbers. After all, for years the sex ratios of livestock have been altered by culling, so that bulls and rams are few and far between. And of course the artificial insemination of humans with fresh sperm is no longer a rarity. With increasing male redundancy, sex selection would only become an additional minor complication and an inevitable extension of the technology. All this seems rather far-fetched at the moment, but until recently so did landing on the moon. Does this mean that the persistent prevalence of son preference would at last be replaced by the dawn of daughter preference? Some would regard this as highly desirable, and an antidote to the excessive aggressiveness of male-dominated activities in the modern world. Social dynamism is so rapid and so lacking in a natural pattern that such a scenario is certainly feasible, even if improbable in certain modern societies.

The possible implications of sex selection are phenomenal, but should be seen in the wider context of the completion of the Human Genome Project at the beginning of the twenty-first century, which will enable a considerable reduction in the 5000 or so genetic disorders and usher in an age when humans will increasingly become objects of conscious design. Greater choice to have more 'perfect children' will become available to the 'haves' in both rich and poor countries alike, but one likely effect will be for the gap between the 'haves' and the 'have-nots' to grow wider still. Of course, genetic modification will not be all plain sailing, for geneticists are constantly surprised by the unexpected results of their research, and there are real worries that by tinkering with human genes nightmare scenarios might result. Rapid scientific advances imply enormous possible implications for the compositions and structures of populations during the twenty-first century, but the recent public outcry about the production of genetically modified crops in the United Kingdom indicate that these issues are going to be of growing concern.

CHAPTER 4

MORE MALE DEATHS

4.1 Sex Ratios of Deaths

Males do not live as long as females, and therefore have higher death rates. Sex ratios of deaths are affected not only by the death rates of the two sexes, but also by their relative numbers in a population. Consequently, they vary much more around the world than sex ratios of births. But except in those developing countries where females are seriously disadvantaged, sex ratios of deaths are commonly in excess of 100, because male death rates are usually (but not always) higher than female death rates at almost every age, and the gap between the rates tends to grow with age. Consequently, the sex ratios of deaths tend to reduce the overall sex ratios of most populations. As couples are having fewer children world-wide and they are surviving longer, the older age groups are accounting for a growing proportion of total populations, and as women generally outlive men these ageing populations inevitably tend to comprise an increasing proportion of older women.

It should not be surprising that sex ratios of deaths in many MDCs are particularly high (over 125), as for example in Canada and Australia, but there they are decreasing and in the United Kingdom the number of female deaths exceeds that of males, because elderly females outnumber elderly males. Sex ratios of deaths are much lower (100–105) in many LDCs, as for example in the Middle East and South Asia where female disadvantage is strong. However, there is no sharp, clear-cut difference in sex ratios of deaths between MDCs and LDCs. The picture is much more complex. Variations in sex-differential mortality are not explained merely by economic status; differences in age-sex structures of populations and cultural factors relating to gender status and roles also have to be taken into account, to the extent that it is often referred to as gender-differential mortality. Whatever the terminology, it will be useful to explain some of the contrasts and similarities in the differential mortality of

MDCs and LDCs, because for better or worse this dualism remains with us, but we should take note of the exceptions.

4.2 The Influence of Sex and Gender on Deaths

Why are male death rates normally higher than those of females? The main reason usually given is that females are naturally more biologically resilient than males in most environmental circumstances, an advantage revealed particularly in their slightly but consistently lower *infant mortality* (i.e. deaths in the first year) and especially *neonatal mortality* (i.e. deaths in the first month) in almost every country, and also their lower *child mortality* (i.e. deaths in the first four years) in all countries where young girls suffer no considerable neglect. Genetic differences play a part, males being biologically more susceptible to most diseases. Carrying only one X chromosome may be a disadvantage to males, as may very high levels of testosterone which are linked to the incidence of prostate cancer and cardiovascular disease. Oestrogen, on the other hand, is thought to protect women against cardiovascular disease and to affect immune functioning, and they also have a stronger antibody response to viral illnesses but are more susceptible to auto-immune diseases such as rheumatoid arthritis (Pollard and Hyatt, 1999: 6; Vallin, 1999: 3-6).

However, socio-cultural factors play a very important part. Gender roles lead to different health risks, behaviours when ill, and levels of care (Pollard and Hyatt, 1999). Male behaviour leads to higher mortality, through the way males live their lives, particularly as younger adults when male mortality tends to peak. Men have a greater ability to self-destruct, by warfare, conflicts and accidents of all types, by not looking after their health as well as women, and by being much more prone to obesity and to common addictions such as smoking, drinking, alcoholism and drugs, all facilitated by their greater access to disposable income. Even male suicide rates are higher at all ages, but especially among younger adults, although obviously the numerical effect of suicides on general mortality rates is small, despite the rapid rise in suicides in some countries, notably Japan and Russia. According to WHO, of the 51 million people or so who die each year only about half a million commit suicide, about 1%. All of these gender roles and activities tend to widen the innate sex-differential in mortality.

In most societies throughout human history men have enjoyed more dominant roles and women have suffered more subordinate roles, so that women's natural advantages in longevity have been offset by their lowlier status (Vallin, 1999: 7-9). In recent decades, that persistent patriarchal tradition has undergone some profound changes, particularly in many of the more developed countries. In most parts of the world, women are now living longer, healthier lives, are marrying later and having less children, are better fed, educated and employed, and have more rights than ever before (Neft and Levine, 1997). They are also enjoying or being subjected to more medicalisation, because normal female functions (e.g. menstruation, menopause, childbirth, lactation) are being treated more and more as medical problems (Pollard and Hyatt, 1999: 7). Of course, the picture is very uneven, and this unevenness has had a marked effect on differential mortality of males and females around the world.

Apart from the impact of excessive maternal mortality during the reproductive age groups in LDCs with limited medical facilities, female mortality is now generally lower than male mortality at all ages, but it has not always been so. This innate sex-differential is variously affected by gender roles in different societies from time to time and from culture to culture, so that males fare much better in some societies than in others and likewise the situation of females is highly variable. Consequently, sex ratios of mortality have varied considerably over time and space, and sometimes female mortality has been unusually high. In Europe, for example, women have not always been so favoured in the mortality stakes as they are today. Witch-hunts during the sixteenth and seventeenth centuries are said to have killed some 16 million women (Bandarage, 1997: 122), and even in the nineteenth century it was common for female death rates to be higher than male death rates in childhood, adolescence and in early adulthood, as they are in some South Asian countries today. Moreover, the increasing technological ability to wreak mass destruction in modern warfare means that during the twentieth century warfare has become less sex-selective than in the past. Bombs are less sex-selective than bullets. Nevertheless, the young adult male cohorts are always most affected; to such an extent in West Germany in 1946 after the Second World War that the sex ratio of the age group 20–39 years was only 63. Younger men have also worked in more dangerous, strenuous and stressful occupations, so the recent falls in occupational risks through better working conditions in various parts of the world have generally benefited men more than women (Retherford, 1975), but that benefit has not been enough to transform the overall pattern of sex-differential mortality partly because women look after themselves better (Vallin, 1999: 19-22).

The preponderance of male deaths obviously tends to diminish the overall sex ratios of populations, thus continually counteracting the preponderance of male births. Initial declines in overall death rates tend to benefit especially male infants and children, who are most vulnerable, and consequently they delay the age when the numbers of females in a population catch up with the numbers of males. Ulizzi and Zonta (1994), analysing stillbirth rates and infant mortality rates in the USA over a period of 50 years, came to the conclusion that sex-differential mortality at early ages was disappearing over time, with males drawing a greater advantage than females from the improved living conditions. Now the sex ratio in one-year old infants is similar to that observed at birth. The male and female child mortality rates of the United States had converged so that in 1996 they were 12 and 9 per thousand respectively, while those of the United Kingdom were 9 and 7.

Reduction in infant and child mortality in **Britain** has also had important effects in this respect. In 1911, when infant and child mortality were both especially high among boys, parity in the numbers of males and females was attained as early as age 6, after which females outnumbered males increasingly with age. It was said to be a factor accounting for the considerable number of unmarried women at the time; spinster aunts were common in many families. Since then, reduction in male mortality, despite the devastating impact of two world wars, has meant that parity in the numbers of males and females has been delayed considerably and is not now reached until the mid-40s to mid-50s age groups. After then, with men's mortality disadvantage rising in their 60s more than in most European countries (Hart, 1989), female preponderance increases rapidly, although of course both sexes are now living longer. These changes are reflected in the contrasting sex ratios of quinquennial age groups in England and Wales between 1911 and 1981 (Table 4.1).

The pattern of sex-differential mortality within populations varies throughout life. In most countries male mortality is much higher than female mortality among the older age groups, and in some countries (e.g. Australia and Canada) the male mortality rates for certain age groups are twice as high. In England and Wales, the age gap in mortality between men and women does not

Table 4.1   Sex Ratios of Age Groups of the Population of England & Wales, 1911 and 1981 (Population in thousands)

Age Group	1911			1981		
	Males	Females	*Sex Ratio*	Males	Females	*Sex Ratio*
0–4	1936	1918	*101*	1492	1418	*105*
5–9	1847	1850	*100*	1647	1560	*106*
10–14	1748	1752	*100*	1972	1874	*105*
15–19	1655	1682	*98*	2054	1966	*104*
20–24	1503	1673	*89*	1805	1760	*103*
25–29	1456	1623	*90*	1646	1627	*101*
30–34	1376	1501	*92*	1834	1821	*101*
35–39	1261	1352	*93*	1554	1538	*101*
40–44	1075	1158	*93*	1405	1387	*101*
45–49	926	1000	*93*	1351	1338	*101*
50–54	768	834	*92*	1381	1404	*98*
55–59	608	670	*91*	1403	1674	*84*
60–64	477	543	*85*	1196	1337	*89*
65–69	366	441	*83*	1100	1326	*83*
70–74	237	317	*75*	871	1191	*73*
75–79	128	183	*70*	544	914	*56*
80 +	79	129	*61*	368	960	*38*

Source: Mitchell, B.R. (1998) *International Historical Statistics: Europe 1750–1993*, Macmillan Reference Ltd., London, 4th ed., 41–2.

change greatly after age 40, so that older men have death rates similar to women five years older (Craig, 1995).

4.3   The Gender Gap in Life Expectancy

Both men and women are living much longer than ever before. Life expectancy at birth of the world population massively improved by 17–18 years during the second half of the twentieth century, and that improvement is forecast to continue. Average life expectancy at birth for the world population as a whole rose from about 46 for males and 49 for females in 1950, a gender gap of 3 years, to 63.4 years for males and 67.7 for females in 1996, a gender gap of 4.3 years. But the widening of the gender gap was much greater in MDCs than in LDCs. In MDCs, average male life expectancy at birth rose from 63.3 in 1950 to 70.6 in 1996 while comparable female life expectancy rose from 68.6 to 78.4, so the gender gap increased from 5.3 years to 7.8. In LDCs, the life expectancy gains were greater but the gap remained much smaller; average life expectancy at birth for males rising from only 41.3 to 62.1, while that for females rose from 43.1 to 65.2, so the gender gap increased from only 1.8 years to 3.1, but in LLDCs it was still only 2.1 years (UNFPA, 1998). Of course, these are fairly crude estimates, but the fact is that women live longer than men in almost all countries, and as life expectancy for the two sexes rises the gap between male and female life expectancy also generally increases. It is also one of the paradoxes that as the status of women improves their advantage over men in longevity grows.

Wide gender differences in life expectancy at birth are seen at continental and sub-continental levels, and generally the gender gap is growing (see Table 4.2), although exceptions are found in parts of Africa, Oceania and North America. The extremes are found in Eastern Europe, where the average gender gap in the 1990s exceeded 10 years through marked male disadvantage in life expectancy, and in South-Central Asia, where until the late 1990s it was either negative or less than a year through strong female disadvantage. But between the two extremes there is a wide range which broadly reflects considerable world-wide cultural disparities.

The gender gap of life expectancy at birth at national level varies even more; in 1996 it was as wide as 13.5 years in favour of women in Russia, but as narrow as 0.5 years in favour of men in Nepal. As we shall see, Russia is characteristic of a number of other East European countries, especially those that were former western republics of the USSR (Estonia, Latvia, Lithuania, Belarus and Ukraine), where the gender gap rose to 10 years or more during the 1990s largely through men faring worse than in previous years. At the other end of the spectrum, the gender gap in life expectancy is only 1–2 years in many African countries and even less in some South Asian countries (e.g. India, Bangladesh

Table 4.2   Life Expectancy at Birth according to Sex by Major Area and Region, 1970–95

Major Area & Region	1970–75			1990–95		
	Males	Females	Gap	Males	Females	Gap
World	56.4	59.4	**3**	62.2	66.5	**4.3**
MDCs	67.6	74.7	**7.1**	70.4	78	**7.6**
LDCs	53.9	55.4	**1.5**	60.6	63.7	**3.1**
LLDCs	*42.8*	*44.5*	*1.7*	*48.7*	*50.8*	*2.1*
Africa	**44.5**	**47.6**	**3.1**	**50.4**	**53.3**	**2.9**
Eastern Africa	43.2	46.4	**3.2**	45.4	48	**2.6**
Central Africa	42.3	45.6	**3.3**	49.3	52.7	**3.4**
Northern Africa	50	52.6	**2.6**	60.8	63.4	**2.6**
Southern Africa	50.6	56.3	**5.7**	59.3	64.9	**5.6**
Western Africa	41.4	44.4	**3**	48	51.1	**3.1**
Asia	**55.8**	**56.8**	**1**	**63.2**	**66**	**2.8**
Eastern Asia	63.2	65.2	**2**	67.6	71.9	**4.3**
South-Central Asia	50.8	49.6	**−1.2**	59.9	60.8	**0.9**
South-Eastern Asia	50.3	53.5	**3.2**	61.7	65.6	**3.9**
Western Asia	56.1	59.9	**3.8**	64.4	68.4	**4**
Europe	**67.1**	**74.2**	**7.1**	**68.5**	**76.9**	**8.4**
Eastern Europe	64.8	73.4	**8.6**	63	73.6	**10.6**
Northern Europe	69.2	75.5	**6.3**	71.9	78	**6.1**
Southern Europe	68.7	74.2	**5.5**	72.9	79.3	**6.4**
Western Europe	68.4	75	**6.6**	73.2	80.2	**7**
Latin America & Caribbean	**58.7**	**63.5**	**4.8**	**65.3**	**71.8**	**6.5**
Caribbean	61.4	65	**3.6**	66.4	70.8	**4.4**
Central America	59	63.7	**4.7**	67.6	73.4	**5.8**
South America	58.3	63.3	**5**	64.4	71.4	**7**
North America	**67.7**	**75.4**	**7.7**	**72.8**	**79.5**	**6.7**
Oceania	**64**	**69.4**	**5.4**	**70.3**	**75.6**	**5.3**
Australia & New Zealand	68.4	75.1	**6.7**	74.5	80.3	**5.8**

Source: UN, 1996.

and Nepal) where women fare much worse than they should do, and where males have always enjoyed a longer life expectancy than females.

It will not have escaped notice that these two groups of countries at either end of the spectrum of gender gaps in life expectancy at birth are among those with the highest and lowest population sex ratios listed in Table 2.3, indicating that sex-differential mortality plays a very important part in influencing population sex ratios. In Figure 4.1, countries with high and low gender gaps in life expectancy at birth of 8 or more years and 2.5 years or less are plotted against their overall sex ratios, and the correlation is clear. These two groups of countries are depicted in map form in Figure 4.2.

4.4   Sex-Differential Mortality in More Developed Countries

In MDCs, male mortality is generally higher than female mortality at all age groups and for most causes of death, and in the majority of countries women on

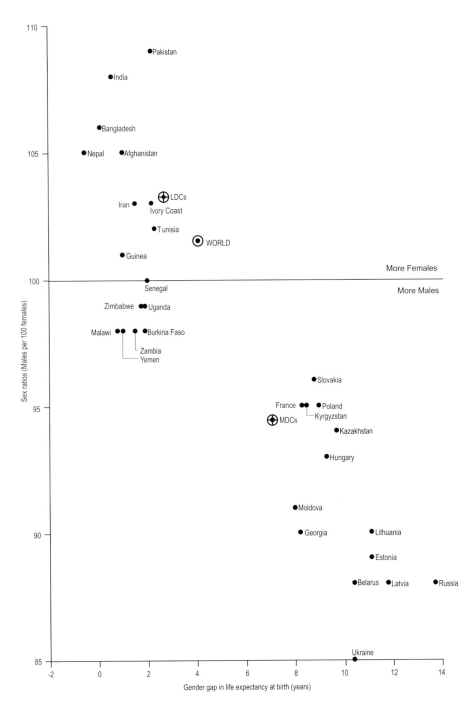

Figure 4.1 Sex ratio and gender gap in life expectancy of countries with high and low gender gaps.

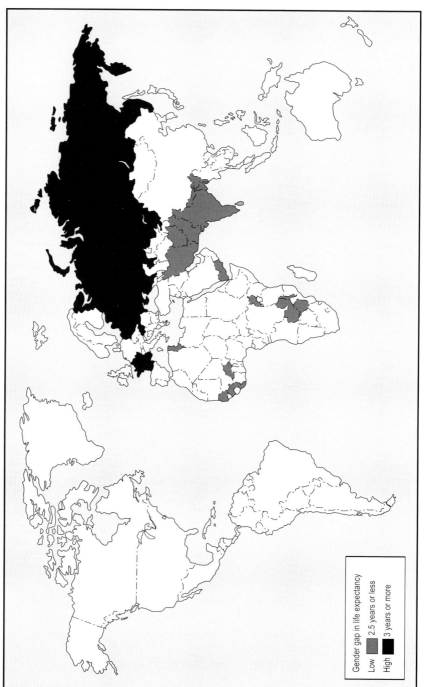

Figure 4.2   World map of large and small gender gaps in life expectancy at birth, mid-1990s.

average outlive men by 5–9 years. There are even notable exceptions where the gender gap in life expectancy at birth is much greater, as mentioned above in relation to some East European countries that were formerly part of the Soviet Union. A more or less gradual widening of the gender differential has been a characteristic feature of mortality trends in MDCs during the twentieth century. At the beginning of the century, the gap in average life expectancy at birth was only 2–3 years, but by 1950 it was 5.3 years, and that gap grew to 7.8 by 1996. The MDCs as a group are expected to maintain continued gradual improvement in life expectancy at birth throughout the first quarter of the twenty-first century, with average life expectancy of males reaching 76.0 by 2025 and females 82.1. This forecast gender gap of 6.1 years is slightly less than at present, largely because of the expected effects of faster progress in reducing the mortality of older men and of the absence of major wars in recent decades.

It will be seen that average *female life expectancy at birth* has risen much faster than that of males in developed countries, so that it now exceeds 80 years in many major countries, namely Japan and France (82.9 years in 1996), Canada and Switzerland (81.8), Spain (81.5), Italy (81.4), Australia (81.2), Belgium, Greece, Netherlands, Norway and Sweden (80.6), Austria, Finland and USA (80.1). The average life expectancy of Japanese and French women is longer than that of the women of any other major country, but many countries press on their heels, female life expectancy being 78 or 79 years in Germany, the United Kingdom, Ireland, New Zealand, Portugal and Denmark, and in most of these countries it should reach 80 years well within a decade.

In contrast, the slower rise in average *male life expectancy at birth* has meant that in only a few developed countries had it reached 75 years by 1996: Japan (76.9), Sweden (76.2), Canada (76.1), Greece (75.5), Australia (75.4), Switzerland (75.3), Italy (75.1) and Netherlands (75.0). Japan is once again leader of the pack. But even in these countries male life expectancy is well outpaced by female life expectancy gains and the gender gap is still about 5–6 years. Male life expectancy in most MDCs has still not advanced beyond the high 60s or lower 70s. Indeed, in some MDCs (e.g. United States, Australia, Netherlands) there was little or no improvement in male life expectancy during several decades after the middle of the century, although it did pick up subsequently. In the United Kingdom, the gap between average male and female life expectancy widened over the decade 1986–96 reaching 5.3 years, with life expectancy of males 74.5 and that of females 79.8, and was widest in the more deprived areas of the country (Raleigh and Kiri, 1997). Two rather disparate countries with high female and male life expectancies at birth are Japan with 126 million people in 1998 and the second largest economy in the world, and Greece with only 11 million people and 33rd in the world economic ranking.

The progress of **Japan** during the second half of the twentieth century to world leadership in this sphere, with a gender gap of 6 years, is due to a remarkably rapid and simultaneous combination (rather than the more common successive combination) of the two phases of the so-called 'epidemiological transition': declines of deaths from infectious diseases and of deaths of the elderly (Wilmoth, 1998). This world leadership in life expectancy at birth owes something to the great surge in economic development since mid-century but is also related to a number of other factors, such as the physical size of Japanese imposing less strain on their hearts, the low fat levels in their diets until the recent introduction of Western eating habits, and, as far as women are concerned, the fact that smoking has long been regarded as unfeminine. On the downside, the social and medical costs of population ageing are expected to reduce economic growth in Japan during the early part of the twenty-first century.

Comparable and to some perhaps surprising longevity occurs in **Greece**, which by 1996 was near the top of the table in both female and male life expectancy at birth with 80.6 and 75.5 years respectively, a gender gap of 5.1 years. Unlike Japan, this status cannot be greatly attributable to economic development, but is perhaps more attributable to the traditional Mediterranean diet of fruit, vegetables, pulses, olive oil and fish, which play a leading role in reducing heart disease, and no doubt to the mildness of the Mediterranean winters. Some of the Greek islands are remarkable in the longevity stakes. The small Aegean island of Simi, north of Rhodes off the coast of Turkey, which had 23,000 people in 1912 but has now a much reduced population of only 2,700, is said to boast at least 40 centenarians, mostly women and proportionately more than anywhere else in Europe. Not surprisingly, it now attracts foreign residents and holiday-makers hoping to emulate the locals.

A much less favourable situation has occurred in Eastern European countries especially those of the former Soviet Union, where dramatic gains in life expectancy at birth after the devastating effects of the Stalinist era (e.g. forced labour camps) and the huge losses of the Second World War were not sustained. During the post-communist 1990s both male and female life expectancies, especially the former, fell sharply, leading to very wide gender gaps of more than 10 years (Table 4.3). These falls have resulted in a marked contrast with the mortality conditions prevailing in Western Europe, where the sex-differential life expectancy at birth is more like 7–9 years (Coleman, 1996). In Eastern Europe, the main problem has been a rise in the mortality of middle aged and older men, many of them having been affected by the appalling conditions of the Stalinist era and the Second World War, although at the same time male infant mortality has generally fallen. The life expectancy for men is worst in the former USSR, where there is now a problem of millions of 'missing men'. In the mid-1990s, male life expectancy at birth was only 63–65 years in most East European republics of the former Soviet Union (e.g. Belarus, Estonia, Latvia, Lithuania

Table 4.3 Countries with Large Estimated Gender Gaps (8 years or more) in Life Expectancy at Birth, 1996

Country	Male L.E.	Female L.E.	Gender Gap	Overall Sex Ratio
Russia	58	71.5	**13.5**	88
Latvia	62.5	74.3	**11.8**	88
Estonia	63.9	75	**11.1**	89
Lithuania	64.9	76	**11.1**	90
Belarus	64.4	74.8	**10.4**	88
Ukraine	63.6	74	**10.4**	85
Kazakhstan	62.8	72.5	**9.7**	94
Hungary	64.5	73.8	**9.3**	93
Poland	66.7	75.7	**9**	95
Slovakia	67	75.8	**8.8**	96
Kyrgyzstan	63.4	71.9	**8.5**	95
France	74.6	82.9	**8.3**	95
Georgia	68.5	76.7	**8.2**	90
Moldova	63.5	71.5	**8**	91

Source: UNFPA (1998) 100–9.

and Ukraine), very low indeed for so-called MDCs and 10–11 years less than female life expectancies which were at the far from unreasonable levels of 74–76 years. Most of these countries are of course expecting overall population declines over the next two decades through low fertility, relatively high mortality and emigration. In a number of other East European countries, namely Hungary, Poland, Slovakia, Georgia, Moldova, Bulgaria, Romania and Finland, male life expectancy is a little better than in the former Soviet republics but female life expectancy is much the same, giving a gender gap of 7–8 years.

Russia, with a large and very slowly declining population of 147 million in 1998, is the extreme example of sex-differential life expectancy, male life expectancy at birth having recently dropped sharply to levels below even the average for LDCs, and well below some of the more demographically advanced LDCs. Now 66th in the UN league table of human development, Russia is also well below many of them (e.g. South Korea, Argentina, Malaysia) in that list. Unusually, this fall in life expectancy has happened during a period of peacetime (Anderson, 1997). In Russia, male life expectancy actually slumped from 64.9 years in 1987, its peak, to only 56.5 in 1996, when female life expectancy was still as high as 70.3, giving a massive gender gap of 13.8 years (see Figure 4.3). Surplus male mortality is especially great (2.5 to 4.5 times) among younger and middle-aged adults between the ages of 20 and 60, leading to a great excess of women over the age of 50 as seen in Figure 4.4. The recent rise in mortality and the gender gap are quite perplexing and do not arise from a single cause (Avdeev *et al.*, 1997). It means that women over the age of 50 greatly exceed men, as seen in the population pyramid for 1997 (Figure 4.4). Analyses of

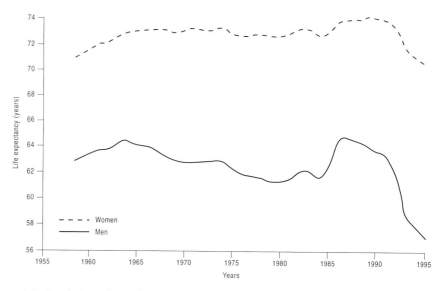

Figure 4.3   Evolution of Russian life expectancy at birth, 1960–96. *Source*: Anderson (1997).

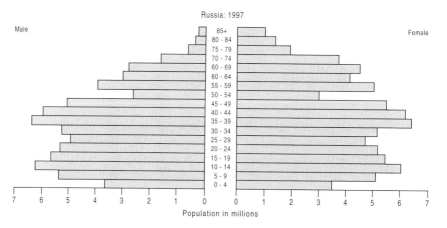

Figure 4.4   Population pyramid for Russia, 1997. *Source*: U.S. Bureau of Census, *International Data Base*.

the causes of the fall in male life expectancy and of the gender gap tend to attribute most of the blame to a variety of factors which appear to act in combination, so that they are not easily dissociated one from another:

- Heavy tobacco smoking leads to high rates of lung cancer, strokes and heart attacks – about 60% of men smoke, compared with less than 10% of women.

- A high incidence of alcoholism, which is also mainly a male affliction, is associated with high rates of poisonings, cirrhosis of the liver, cardio-vascular disease, industrial and other accidents and murders. On average, about a fifth of family incomes is spent on alcohol.
- Severe environmental pollution occurs, especially in the past and present heavy industrial areas. The old mining, iron and steel and chemical industries of the former Soviet Union have been mainly responsible, as for example the infamous coal mining centre of Vorkuta in northern Siberia which employed slave labour during the Stalinist period. More recently, in 1986 the Chernobyl nuclear disaster alone exposed more than 5 million people to radiation, mostly within Ukraine.
- Institutional breakdown and restructuring is associated with the collapse of communism and difficulties in the introduction of the market system, deepening socio-economic crises, widespread unemployment and poverty, and a creaking health care system that suffers from considerable shortages of medicines and medical supplies.
- Psychosocial stress and some social collapse is linked with the above-mentioned factors, connected to a marked rise in the number of suicides and homicides during the 1990s, mostly affecting men. In 1995, there were 42 suicides per 100,000 inhabitants in Russia, twice the rate in France and six times that in the United Kingdom. There were also 45,000 homicides, four-fifths men, and at a very high rate of 32 per 100,000 inhabitants, compared with 9 in the USA, 1 in France and only 0.7 in the United Kingdom. Not surprisingly, the violent death rate in Russia of 209 per 100,000 inhabitants is very much higher than the comparable rates in France (73), USA (56) and the United Kingdom (28) (Chesnais, 1999).

Individually, these various problems have been replicated to a greater or lesser extent in all the much smaller populations of the other East European countries that were former republics of the USSR, with similar demographic effects. In such a vast country as the Russian Federation, they also vary regionally, being influenced not only by economic progress but also by climatic variations; sex-differential mortality tends to be greater in the colder north of Russia and in Siberia than in the milder south and in the Muslim areas. Indeed, it is much less marked in the Central Asian and Transcaucasian republics of the former Soviet Union, especially where Muslim populations are prevalent and where women fare less well but men rather better than in Russia; consequently, in Tajikistan, Turkmenistan and Uzbekistan the gender gap in life expectancy at birth was only 6 to 7 years in 1996 (UNFPA, 1998).

Keen readers will have noticed that **France** appears as the odd country out in Table 4.3 among the list of East European and ex-Soviet countries with large gender gaps in life expectancy due to unusually high male mortality. It does so largely because its current gender gap of 8.3 years arises from a good average male life expectancy (74.6 years in 1996) for a West European country, in spite of the negative impacts of two world wars, accompanied by an exceptionally high female life expectancy (82.9), which along with Japan is the highest in the world. France has made remarkable progress in reducing both male and female mortality, but as women have benefited more than men the gender gap in life expectancy at birth has grown fairly consistently during the twentieth century; it was 3.4 years in 1900, 5.7 in the early 1930s and 7.6 in 1969. In the past, many of the reasons given above for the shorter life span of men in Russia have also been stressed in the case of Frenchmen: excessive consumption of alcohol, tobacco and rich food, too many suicides and traffic fatalities, the less attentive attitude of men to their health and their lower consumption of medicines – all these on top of their lower biological durability. Obviously, the causes of contrasting male and female longevity are complex, but the striking durability of Frenchwomen has been attributed partly to the way that their behaviour patterns contrast markedly and increasingly with those of Frenchmen, and partly to the fact that they have profited more than men from substantial progress in the fight against cardiovascular diseases and cancer (Meslé and Vallin, 1998). It should also be emphasised that France is not totally exceptional among West European countries in respect of its gender gap in life expectancy at birth; Belgium, Portugal and Spain all have gender gaps of 7 or 7.1 years.

Looking at MDCs in general, infant and child mortality are already relatively low, mortality of the under 5s during 1990-95 averaging 15 per thousand for boys and 11 per thousand for girls, and being as low as 7 and 6 per thousand respectively in several Scandinavian countries: Finland, Norway and Sweden (UNFPA, 1998). Life expectancy gains occur mainly among older age groups, usually now categorised as those aged 65 and over, including those sometimes called the 'young old' aged 65–79 and the 'oldest old' either 75 and over or 80 and over – although definitions and terms vary. Older age mortality rates are declining in most MDCs, rather more rapidly for women than for men, and in very many countries, including the United Kingdom and most countries of the European Union, the death rates of women aged 80–84 are at least 20–25% lower than those of men of the same age. On the other hand, the gap is less marked among older men and women aged 85 and over, but it should be noted that in no European country have the 85-plus year olds so far reached 2% of the total population (or 1% in Eastern Europe).

Unfortunately, life expectancy does not coincide with healthy life expectancy, sometimes called 'active life expectancy' or 'disease-free life expectancy' (US Bureau of Census, 1992). Amongst the MDCs, there is a greater range in healthy life expectancy than in life expectancy in general. In some MDCs such as the

United Kingdom, the proportion of life expectancy without moderate or light disability has diminished, while the proportion without severe disability remains stable. On the whole, women can expect more years of ill-health than men later in life and to live much longer than men in a state of severe handicap or in a disabled state. The visual evidence is all too clear today in our nursing and residential homes, where older incapacitated women greatly outnumber older men.

4.5 Sex-Differential Mortality in Less Developed Countries

The situation is very different in most of the LDCs. In general, with much greater mortality than MDCs at mid-century, they have enjoyed fairly widespread and continuous improvement in life expectancy during the second half of the twentieth century, although with a much smaller sex-differential. Thus, in 1950, when there was a marked contrast between the demographic dynamics and characteristics of MDCs and LDCs as groups of countries, the average life expectancy at birth in the LDCs was still very low at 41.3 years for males and 43.1 for females, and the gender gap was only 1.8 years. The subsequent progress in demographic transition that occurred in most LDCs, especially through lowering mortality, was so strong and widespread during the second half of the twentieth century that by 1996 average life expectancies at birth had risen to 62.1 years for males and 65.2 for females, a wider gender gap of 3.1 years that is expected to carry on widening during the early decades of the twenty-first century to reach about 4.2 years by 2025. At that time, the national gender gaps of life expectancy in most LDCs will probably be of the order of 3–6 years, but still less than we find in most MDCs even today.

On the whole, the gains in life expectancy in LDCs have resulted more from improvements in infant and child mortality rates, arising especially from declines in the impact of infectious diseases, rather than in the longevity gains at older ages that are so typical today of MDCs. The sex-differential in life expectancy at birth is lower in most LDCs because many girls and women do not enjoy as good living conditions or survive as well as they should do, and consequently, as we shall see later in this chapter, older women do not outnumber older men to the same extent as in MDCs.

As LDCs have experienced varying levels and rates of demographic transition from high to low fertility and mortality and are becoming increasingly diverse demographically, sex-differential mortality now varies substantially among them. In some of the developing countries which have experienced considerable mortality decline, as for example Singapore, Taiwan, Israel, Kuwait, United Arab Emirates, Costa Rica, Mexico, Puerto Rico, Cuba, Jamaica, Trinidad and Tobago and several South American countries (Argentina, Chile, Uruguay, Venezuela), female life expectancy at birth now exceeds 75 years and in some it is approaching 80 years, higher than in many MDCs. In Puerto Rico it was 80.5 in 1996. Israel is of course a somewhat unusual case of a so-called developing country; in 1996 average life expectancy at birth of females was 79.5 and that of males 75.7, a gap of 3.8 years, but for the Arab population of Israel the gap was only 1.5 years, the respective life expectancies being 75.7 and 74.2. Inevitably, the situation often varies geographically within a country; for example, in Argentina (where the life expectancy of a female is 76.8 and that of a male 69.6, a gap of 7.2 years) a woman in Buenos Aires may expect to live 9 years longer than in one the rural provinces, and a man 7 years more.

Sri Lanka is an example of a quite densely peopled South Asian country, with 18 million people in 1998, which has transformed its sex-differential mortality despite being low in the economic league tables (Nadarajah, 1983). Back in 1920–22, male life expectancy at birth was only 32.7 years and that of females 30.7, a gender gap of 2 years in favour of males. By 1958 these average life expectancies had risen to 59.8 and 58.8 respectively, still a gap of one year in favour of males. But in the early 1960s the differential began to favour females and that process has continued so strongly that by 1996 average male life expectancy at birth was 70.9 but that of females had risen as high as 75.4, a gender gap of 4.5 years with life expectancies that would be envied by many MDCs. Nadarajah pointed out that the gain for females had been right across the board; whereas in 1952–54 males had lower death rates than females at all ages from 1 to 44 and again after 75, by 1970–72 they had higher death rates at all ages except 1 to 9 when higher female mortality in childhood resulted mainly from the persistence of son preference. The main reason for the overall reduction in female mortality was a drop in maternal mortality; it accounted directly for about 40% of female mortality reduction and also helped indirectly.

The situation is very different in some other South Asian, Middle Eastern and African countries, where demographic transition is less advanced, especially where patriarchal societies prevail and where male preference, high fertility and substantial female neglect combine to reduce female longevity so much that excess female mortality extends over many age groups from childhood (not infancy) to old age. Consequently the gender gap in life expectancy at birth is often reduced to a year or two, or even in the case of Nepal it disappears (see Table 4.4). Nepal is not alone, but one of a number of poor countries where life expectancy at birth has been sometimes higher for men than for women. Recent estimates for 1996 are that it was 57.6 for men in comparison with 57.1 for women (much higher than in 1970, when the comparable figures were 43 and 42), a reflection of the fact that women do most of the farm and house work, have now an average of 4.9 children and receive less health care and

Table 4.4   Countries with Small Estimated Gender Gaps (2.5 years or less) in Life Expectancy at Birth, 1996

Country	Male L.E.	Female L.E.	Gender Gap	Overall Sex Ratio
Tunisia	68.4	70.7	**2.2**	102
Pakistan	62.9	65.1	**2.2**	109
Ivory Coast	50	52.2	**2.2**	103
Senegal	50.3	52.3	**2**	100
Burkina Faso	45.1	47	**1.9**	98
Uganda	40.4	42.3	**1.9**	99
Zimbabwe	47.6	49.4	**1.8**	99
Iran	68.5	70	**1.5**	103
Zambia	42.2	43.7	**1.5**	98
Afghanistan	45	46	**1**	105
Guinea	46	47	**1**	101
Yemen	57.4	58.4	**1**	98
Malawi	40.3	41.1	**0.8**	98
India	62.1	62.7	**0.6**	108
Bangladesh	58.1	58.2	**0.1**	106
Nepal	57.6	57.1	**−0.5**	105

Source: UNFPA (1998) 100–9.

nutrition than men. This gender gap now also hovers around zero in Bangladesh.

The gender gap in life expectancy at birth is well under a year in **India**, where until about 1985 it was higher for males than for females. Indeed, it remains a year or so in favour of males in some of the large northern states (e.g. Uttar Pradesh, Madhya Pradesh, Orissa and Bihar) that have populations comparable with sizeable countries, but the picture is quite different in peninsular India where there is a gender gap in life expectancy of five years in favour of females in the southern state of Kerala and gaps of two to three years in several other states (e.g.Tamil Nadu, Karnataka, Andhra Pradesh and Maharashtra), reflecting the north/south cultural contrasts in India that have and will be mentioned on several occasions.

Poverty plays an important part in slowing down progress in mortality gains in LDCs and in maintaining a narrow gap between male and female life expectancies. Those 40 poor countries designated as Least Developed (sometimes abbreviated as LLDCs) have not done so well. Mostly located in Sub-Saharan Africa but with the addition of Afghanistan, Cambodia and Haiti, their average life expectancies at birth for males and females were only 50.9 and 53.0 in 1996, far below the average for LDCs, and the gender gap was only 2.1 years. In the majority of these countries, male life expectancy is less than 50 years, while in nearly half of them both male and female life expectancies are less than 50. Neither male nor female life expectancy exceeds 47 years in more than half a dozen of the poorest countries at the bottom of the average life expectancy league tables (and of most other league tables as well): Afghanistan, Burkina Faso, Sierra Leone, Guinea, Guinea-Bissau, Malawi and Burundi. In all of these poor countries the average gender gap in life expectancy at birth is only of the order of 1.0 to 3.3 years.

> In the small West African country of **Sierra Leone**, with less than 5 million inhabitants in 1998, which despite abundant mineral and agricultural resources has suffered so greatly in recent years from ravaging war and civil strife that it is firmly rooted at the bottom of the United Nations league tables of human development, average male and female life expectancies at birth in the mid-1990s were still as low as 36.0 and 39.1 years. It is currently the only country in the world with both levels under 40, although its life expectancy gender gap of 3.1 is unremarkable. It is small consolation that the country has long experienced low life expectancies, and that in the early 1950s during the final years of British colonial rule male and female life expectancies were only 27.6 and 30.4 years respectively.

Many of these LLDCs where the gap between male and female mortality is low suffer from high levels of maternal mortality and female neglect, two topics that we will examine now.

4.6   The Scourge of Maternal Mortality

Although now a rare occurrence in most MDCs, maternal mortality is a still a common phenomenon in the poorer LDCs and LLDCs, where it is one of the main causes of death of women in the reproductive age groups. The risk of dying in childbirth rises with age, women in their forties having five times the maternal death rate of those in their twenties (Potts and Short, 1999: 262–3), so the menopause is a natural check on maternal mortality. WHO has estimated that nearly a million women die in the world each year through complications associated with reproduction, and that in 1996 585,000 deaths were linked to pregnancy and childbirth, many of them as a result of abortions. About 99% of these women live in LDCs, mostly in the poorer countries that are on the whole the least equipped to cope with the problem. Judith Mackay (1993: 90–1) has pointed out that although the risks associated with pregnancy have diminished, the absolute number of births in LDCs has increased, so that the number of women dying in maternity remains relatively stable.

As for so many other social and economic phenomena, the situation is worst in most of the poorer countries of Africa, along with a few of the poorer Asian countries. In some of the poorer African countries even the risks are increasing, and so maternal mortality is much higher than elsewhere. Too many African women are having babies when they are too young, and they are having them too close together, in unhygienic conditions with limited access to clean water, health clinics and modern medical care. As Judith Mackay (1993) has said, "maternal mortality will only diminish when women are better educated, fed and cared for". Too often they suffer from neglect.

The United Nations Organisation (1990) has long emphasised that the five key factors contributing to high levels of maternal mortality are:

- early (teenage) and late pregnancies;
- too closely spaced pregnancies;
- high parity births;
- lack of access to health services, due partly to poor transportation; and
- lack of trained birth attendants.

In addition, the situation is made worse by the poor nutritional status of many mothers, as well as the frequency of poorly performed abortions that are estimated to affect about two in five of all cases of maternal mortality in LDCs (Haider, 1996: 109), and that are often a reflection of the lack of adequate family planning services available at grass roots level. It is also exacerbated by the notorious practice of female circumcision (more commonly now known as female genital mutilation), a form of violence against women found especially in much of north-eastern Africa, that causes many further health problems in pregnancy and childbirth.

Efforts to reduce maternal mortality have not always been successful, partly because they have had to deal with women suffering from acute poverty and partly because they have been almost inseparable from efforts to encourage family limitation and reduce fertility. Thus, the Safe Motherhood Initiative sponsored by various international agencies has sometimes been accused of being more motivated by population control than poverty alleviation, more concerned with sterilisation of women than saving their lives (Bandarage, 1997: 94). Progress in reducing maternal mortality certainly might have been much more successful; it still remains high even in those poor countries where birth rates have fallen substantially. For example, in Bangladesh while fertility declined from 7 to 4 children per woman between 1970 and 1995 maternal mortality remained as high as 850 per 100,000 live births in the mid-1990s. Similarly in India, where fertility has also fallen considerably, maternal mortality was still at the unacceptably high level of 570.

Consequently, maternal mortality rates range massively world-wide. Figure 4.5 reveals that the highest levels are found in Tropical Africa and a few of the poorest countries in Asia. They are estimated to be as appallingly high as 1800 maternal deaths per 100,000 live births in Sierra Leone, 1700 in Afghanistan and 1500–1600 in some other very poor countries, such as Somalia, Guinea, Mozambique, Chad, Angola, Bhutan and Nepal, although obviously in such countries these estimates can only be crude (UNFPA, 1998). At the other end of the range, much more accurate rates of less than 50 per 100,000 are found in

Human Dichotomy

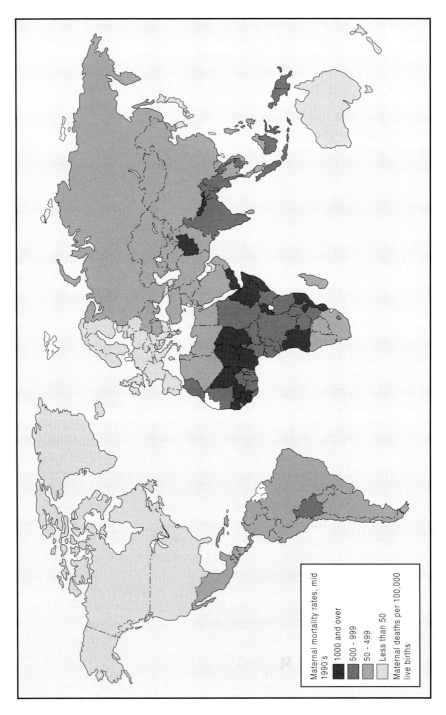

Figure 4.5 World map of maternal mortality rates (maternal deaths per 100,000 live births) of countries of the world, mid-1990s.

nearly all MDCs, and rates of less than 10 per 100,000 are recorded in a number of the wealthier and smaller MDC populations: 6 in Switzerland, Canada and Norway, 7 in Israel, Spain and Sweden, and 9 in Australia, Denmark and the United Kingdom. Pregnant women obviously face vastly different chances of successful confinements and of survival in different parts of the world, there being very little geographical equality in maternal mortality. Some of this inequality results from female neglect.

4.7 The Scandal of Female Neglect

Female neglect, sometimes known as gender bias, has long been a severe problem in many parts of the world, but owing to considerable social and economic progress in many MDCs since the eighteenth century it is most evident today in some of the LDCs. The United Nations Development Programme (UNDP) has concluded that in no country do women fare socio-economically better than men, and that they account for 70% of the world's poor and 66% of its illiterates. Moreover, it is estimated that on average two-thirds of their work is unpaid, compared with only one-third of that of men. These statistical generalisations of the gender gap are intended to give broad brush indications, which are not generally in dispute, but the statistics have certainly been questioned. For example, the estimate that women account for 70% of the world's poor is regarded as implausibly high by Alain Marcoux (1998) who suggests that 55% is more probable – even so, nobody should dispute that the figure is unacceptably high.

Gender bias is highly variable geographically and is multi-dimensional. It differs from country to country and from one aspect of life to another: levels of literacy, education, nutrition, health care, economic activity, employment and income, age of marriage, availability of divorce, domestic roles, ownership of property, political involvement, human rights, etc. On the whole, the plight of women is made worse where they are poor, where patriarchal and fundamentalist societies prevail, and where they are subject to violence and are expected to suffer in silence. Considerable geographical variability in what may for simplicity's sake be called the status of women, a term that is not easily quantified, has great demographic implications because it has profound effects upon fertility, mortality and mobility.

In a number of poorer countries, as for example in the South Asian countries of Afghanistan, Bangladesh, India, Nepal and Pakistan, gender inequality and female subordination are often exacerbated by physical neglect which has a considerable impact on the health, welfare and life expectancy of women (Rousham, 1999). In comparison with boys and men, girls and women have suffered from much lower levels of nutrition, medical attention, education and general care, and these have had a cumulative effect upon the roles of women not only as mothers but also socially, economically and demographically, reducing their ability to cope and causing them to experience much higher levels of morbidity and mortality (Lopez and Ruzicka 1983; Retherford 1975). In such countries, the natural biological advantage of girls and women is severely reduced by the many social disadvantages which they suffer. These are often reflected in higher female mortality after the first month of life, during the post-neonatal period, when the mortality rates of baby girls should be lower than those of baby boys. Consequently, in a few countries (Bangladesh, China, India, Iran, Mongolia, Nepal and Vietnam) we even find the unusual fact that the mortality of boys aged under 5 is actually higher than of girls of a similar age (UNFPA, 1998).

Results from the *Nepal* Family Health Survey, held in 1996, revealed that after the first year of life girls are at a significantly greater risk of dying than boys. Whereas infant mortality is 8% higher for boys, child mortality is 22% higher for girls, suggesting that girls receive less care than boys. Answers to questions about mothers' sex preference confirm a bias against girls; 60% of the children surveyed have mothers who would have preferred only one daughter, and 11% have mothers who did not want a daughter at all.

In *China*, evidence has been found of excessive female mortality at most ages for nearly all cohorts since those born in the late 1930s (Coale and Banister, 1994), but it arises mainly from higher infant and child mortality of girls resulting from shorter breastfeeding and widespread discriminatory practices including less nutrition, general care and health care (Riley and Gardner, 1997). Naturally, hard data are not readily available, and it has been suggested that the deaths of baby girls are more likely to have been missed than those of baby boys.

Sex-differential mortality has been much studied in *India*, where census reports have long revealed shortages of females – the 1991 census indicated that there were only 927 females per 1000 males (using the Indian census practice of expressing sex ratios) – and have generally indicated that this is partly a reflection of female neglect. Unusually for a major country, in India more females than males die in childhood and in early adulthood at ages up to 30, and until the 1980s (as in Pakistan, Bangladesh and Nepal) life expectancy at birth for females was less than that for males. This has long been known, but was confirmed by the 1992–93 National Family Health Survey (NFHS) of India, which revealed that although neonatal (first month) mortality of boys was 14% higher than that of girls, as would be normally expected, thereafter there was an immediate turnaround, postneonatal (1–11 months) mortality being 19% higher for girls than boys, and child (1–4 years) mortality 40% higher for girls.

Female disadvantage in mortality is generally attributed to the relative neglect of girls and younger women; it has been estimated to be four times as important numerically as female infanticide and sex-selective abortions, and Das Gupta and Mari Bhat (1997) have estimated that it may account for about a million excess deaths a year. They have also pointed out that the net effect of fertility decline in India has been an excess mortality of girls relative to that of boys resulting from two countervailing forces, namely (a) the reduction in the number of higher-parity births which reduces net mortality, and (b) the intensity of parity-specific discrimination which increases it.

Female neglect in India is demonstrated in a variety of ways:

- less breastfeeding of baby girls;
- poorer nutrition;
- higher levels of kwashiorkor, stemming from inadequate intake of protein;
- less health and medical care;
- excessive child labour, from which of course boys are not excused;
- early marriage of girls, often aged 14 to 16, and early child-bearing;
- numerous children;
- high maternal mortality; and
- limited education and considerable illiteracy.

All these various factors lead to higher female morbidity and mortality, especially during famines and epidemics and among children of high birth parity (i.e. younger children of large families) (Premi, 1994; Kishor, 1995). Female illiteracy in India has been shown to be closely related to female disadvantage in child survival (Murthi *et al.*, 1995); at the 1991 census there were still 197 million illiterate women in India, despite an increase in the literacy rates of younger women, and male literacy rates exceeded those of females by 28%. Improvement in mothers' education clearly reduces the mortality of children under 5 years, especially that of girls in the northern states. Perhaps surprisingly, female disadvantage in child survival is much lower in districts with higher levels of poverty, where both sexes suffer alike. Moreover, discrimination against girls also tends to be more characteristic among the higher castes, and when there is a reduction of poverty among lower castes discrimination against girls actually increases (Kumar *et al.*, 1997: 2213).

Patrilocal marriage traditions, purdah and the system of dowries in India have also reduced the autonomy of women, whose lot in the past was made even worse if they failed to produce sons. Barren women have been frequently unwanted and divorced. It has been estimated that even in the 1990s more than 7,000 bride or dowry deaths took place every year (Neft and Levine, 1997: 96), the young brides either being murdered or taking their own lives. This often takes place after family pressure when their parents do not meet the dowry payments required by the parents of the groom. In the past, the fate of women was worsened by the Hindu practice of sati (or suttee), in which some widows have voluntarily (although this is a matter of debate) committed suicide by burning themselves on the funeral pyres of their husbands. Rare and isolated incidents still occur of this outlawed practice, prohibited even during Mughal times and suppressed by the British in 1828. They are now much deprecated by the more modern elements of Indian society, notably by feminist groups (Tully, 1991: 210–36).

India has such a vast population that simple demographic generalisations are always unwise. Once again regional and cultural differences reveal themselves by contrasts in the incidence of female neglect, particularly between north and south. As in the case of son preference, female neglect is more common in northern India than in the south, leading to much lower survival rates of young girls in Haryana, Uttar Pradesh, Rajasthan and Madhya Pradesh than in Kerala and much of south-west India. Tim Dyson and Mick Moore (1983) also report on the lower marital fertility, later marriage and greater female autonomy in the south, and they regard female social status as the key to understanding India's demographic situation. Peter Atkins and colleagues (1997) have emphasised that the economic value of women in southern India is significantly higher than in the north owing to their greater labour force participation, so that there is a greater probability of them earning a wage and a reduced cost of rearing girls because dowries are lower. Consequently, care of girls is greater and their status higher in the south. The authors also find that the regional contrasts in the survival of girls are much greater than any contrasts relating to either religious identity or caste. They point to the fact that the differences in survival rates between Christians and Muslims in the south are small, as are the differences between Muslims and Hindus in the north (see also Raju *et al.*, 1997).

Gender bias has become a matter of growing concern in India, and will undoubtedly have many repercussions during the twenty-first century. It is therefore vital that family health programmes aiming to improve mortality levels should pay special attention to the welfare, health care and nutrition of young girls. In order to make rapid progress, the NFHS has recommended that intervention programmes should focus on the following high-risk groups:

- children born less than 24 months after a previous birth;
- children in families where an older sibling has died;
- children born to mothers less than 20 years old;
- children of illiterate mothers;
- children in very poor households;
- children in households whose head is Hindu and belongs to a scheduled caste or scheduled tribe; and
- children in households without access to a flush or pit toilet.

Women in **Bangladesh** also suffer from many of the problems experienced in northern India: excessive malnutrition, poverty, early marriage and numerous pregnancies, and although the government has made some progress in tackling high fertility Bangladeshi women still have no advantage over men in life expectancy at birth, both being about 58 years in the mid-1990s. At mealtimes the women and girls tend to eat last and least, and in poorer families their diets are deficient not only in calories but also in vitamins and minerals (Rousham, 1999). When ill, girls are taught to be compliant and not to complain, so their illnesses are seldom reported, whereas the complaints of boys are listened to and consequently they are taken more to clinics (Haider, 1996: 97). Young girls are also less educated than boys and when they are employed, often in domestic service, they receive lower wages. Not surprisingly in these circumstances and contrary to normal expectations, both infant mortality and child mortality rates for girls exceed those for boys; the under-5 mortality rate for girls was estimated at 109 per 1000 live births during 1990–95 compared with 103 for boys (UNFPA, 1998). Consequently, many of the Bangladeshi girls and women who enter marriage at an early age suffer from frail physique and chronic anaemia, factors leading to frequent miscarriages and prolonged labour, and nearly half of all babies suffer from low birth-weight (Haider, 1996).

The health and longevity of Bangladeshi women is further aggravated by the frequency of domestic violence against them, which is apparently commonplace but (as elsewhere in the world) goes largely unreported. The recently reported high incidence of many horrific acid attacks upon women who do not accede to male desires or commands has instigated an international outcry. It is also reported that "hundreds, if not thousands, of women are killed or driven to suicide each year because their dowries were deemed too meagre", despite government prohibition of the practice of dowries and the introduction of the 1995 Repression Against Women and Children Law which provided for the death penalty for those convicted of involvement in dowry deaths (Neft and Levine, 1997: 208). All this evidence makes it abundantly clear that innumerable girls and women in Bangladesh are seriously neglected and disadvantaged.

In *Pakistan* similar incidences of deep-seated mysogyny are evidenced by thousands of cases of acid and kerosene burning of women accused of adultery or premarital relations. They have been estimated by newspapers to result in about 300 deaths a year. It is usually claimed that such killings are for the honour of the tribe, and, quite wrongly, that it is sanctioned by Muslim sharia law. Unfortunately, in such a male-dominated society the killers are rarely brought to book, and, in sharp contrast, male adulterers frequently escape with only short prison sentences.

Female neglect is far from being confined to those countries mentioned so far. It is a major world-wide problem, too often swept under the carpet and excused under the heading of cultural customs. One can scarcely stress too strongly that considerable improvements in female education and in female social and economic status are vital to overcome the long-standing disadvantages faced by girls and women, not merely in those countries of the Indian sub-continent cited here but in many other LDCs as well as in some of the less advanced East European countries, for example Albania, Bulgaria, Hungary and Romania.

Female education is one obvious way forward. The picture of gender disparities in education in the developing world is of course very uneven, but in very many LDCs, notably in Sub-Saharan Africa, South Asia and parts of the Islamic World, there is a great need to reduce those disparities by more schooling for girls at every level, more 'girl-friendly' facilities and more women teachers. The costs of teaching girls should also be lowered, and parents taught to see the long-term value of female education in delaying the onset of marriage and childbearing and in increasing the labour force participation and economic contribution of women (Population Action International, 1998). In 1995, Yemen, Pakistan, Afghanistan, Benin and Chad had the worst records of gender disparities in education. In stark contrast, some more modernising LDCs, like South Korea, Cuba, the Philippines, Tunisia and Tanzania, have benefited greatly from the elimination of this gender disparity, while some other countries, including Mongolia, Venezuela, Uruguay, South Africa and Sri Lanka, even have a reverse gap, with higher secondary enrolment rates for girls – partly because there are currently fewer job opportunities available to them.

4.8   More Older Women than Men

Because in most countries there tends to be excess male mortality throughout the life cycle and longer female life expectancy, women generally outnumber men in most age cohorts after the 30s or 40s, and that difference typically advances with age (US Bureau of Census, 1992: 46–7). The difference is especially wide in the ageing populations of MDCs, where women are less disadvantaged than they were, live much longer, especially longer than men. In contrast, in many younger LDC populations with broadly based age pyramids, the larger size of younger age cohorts means that there tends to be an absolute surplus of males up to about the age of 60, above which there is usually only a small percentage of older people. In consequence, the age of 60 has often been used in the past to identify older populations on a world-wide basis largely because any higher threshold would incorporate only a tiny proportion of LDC populations. That situation is changing as the total world population aged over 60 is now growing rapidly.

The World Bank (1998) have estimated that in 1996 there were 556 million people aged 60 and over, about 9.6% of the world total, and that there will be more than a billion of this age by 2020. Amongst the world's older population the sex ratio was only about 83 men per 100 women, but the range among countries was very wide, from as low as 50 to 60 in several former Soviet republics (Belarus, Estonia, Kazakhstan, Latvia, Lithuania, Russia and Ukraine) to between 120 and 130 in a number of Islamic countries (Bangladesh, Iran, Jordan and Libya), but rising as high as 161 in Kuwait and 222 in the United Arab Emirates where migrant populations outnumbered nationals. In the United Kingdom it was 76, lower than the world average, although that is a fairly high figure for European countries where the average was only about 61.

Figure 4.6 shows that all the MDCs have below average sex ratios of older people aged 60 and over. However, in MDCs older women and older men are more usually defined as those aged 65 and over. Among older people, this a matter of debate with growing pressure to raise the threshold of definition higher, especially as there is very rapid growth in the numbers of those aged 75 and over, sometimes called the 'oldest old' (but not usually by themselves!). Whatever the definition, older women substantially outnumber older men in most developed countries, particularly when the higher 65-year old threshold is used, and in Europe as a whole the sex ratio of those aged 65 and over is now only about 60 compared with a world average of 75.

It will be seen in Table 4.5 that in MDCs sex ratios decline fairly regularly with age, very low ratios occurring at older ages; for example among those aged 80 and over sex ratios are usually below 50. In England and Wales in 1990 women aged 90 and over outnumbered men by 4.4 to one, and women centenarians outnumbered their male counterparts by 7.6 to one, factors which have risen constantly during this century at the same time as numbers have roughly doubled every ten years (Thatcher, 1992: 416). In some countries that were much affected by losses of men during the Second World War, such as Germany, Austria, Poland and the East European countries of the former Soviet Union, older women aged 65 and over are twice as numerous as older men, in sharp contrast with Greece where male life expectancy is very high and where there are as many as 80 older men per 100 women. Unfortunately, in most MDCs older women are usually not as well off as older men; for instance, the average income of female pensioners aged 65–69 in Britain in 1994 was only 65% of that of the whole population, while that of male pensioners was 73%.

Figure 4.6 and Table 4.5 reveal that the pattern of sex ratios of older people for LDCs is much more complicated, largely influenced by the variable extent of fertility decline and the level of female neglect. In broad terms, the proportions of older people, especially older women, are lower in those world regions that have not experienced substantial fertility decline, such as Africa, South Asia and West Asia, than for example in South East Asia and the Caribbean where much demographic transition has taken place and where female status is rising fast. In short, gender roles influence greatly the relative numbers of older men and women. In some countries, as for example Brazil, sex-differential mortality (the gender gap

Human Dichotomy

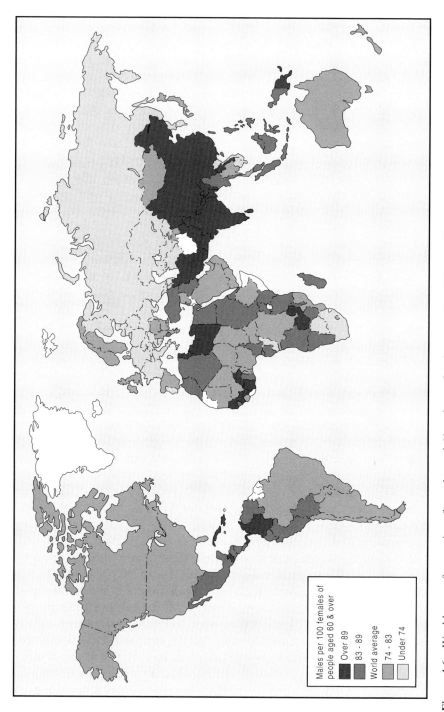

Figure 4.6 World map of sex ratios of people aged 60 and over for the countries of the world, 1996.

Table 4.5 Sex ratios by age of selected populations of countries, circa 1990

Country	25–49	50–64	65–69	70–74	75–79	80 plus
MDCs:						
Australia	103	102	90	80	70	50
Austria	100	92	61	57	52	41
France	101	95	82	75	63	45
Germany	105	97	61	55	48	39
Greece	100	90	88	77	74	69
Italy	100	92	80	72	65	49
Japan	101	95	73	69	66	53
Poland	101	87	70	64	56	44
UK	101	97	85	75	63	43
USA	99	91	81	74	65	46
LDCs:						
Bangladesh	108	115	115	117	132	189
Brazil	99	90	81	76	69	55
China	108	110	98	88	76	56
Colombia	94	89	89	87	79	63
Egypt	101	97	94	95	100	98
India	109	103	101	99	103	117
Pakistan	103	106	109	108	104	105

Source: US Bureau of Census, 1992, *An Aging World II:* 108.

in life expectancy at birth was 7.9 years in 1996) does not differ greatly from that experienced in most MDC populations, with the expectation that women will form an increasing proportion of the older population. On the other hand, in Egypt and some other countries of the Middle East where fertility decline and female status are limited, older women do not outnumber older men so strongly, while in most of the countries of South Asia that are characterised by marked son and male preference, as for example Bangladesh, India and Pakistan, more men than women are reported in almost all older age groups (see Table 4.5).

The growing proportions of older women and the fact that they can expect more years of ill health in later life than men have focused attention on their health problems, particularly by international organisations such as WHO and by the International Year of Older Persons in 1999. Inevitably all older people suffer from increasing ill health, but the greater ill health of older women, especially in those poorer countries where they have unequal access to health services, often arises from past neglect (including domestic violence), malnutrition, specific dietary deficiencies (e.g. vitamin A, zinc, iodine), complicated reproductive histories and their prolonged confinement and restriction within unhygienic homes with smoky kitchens, inadequate toilets and polluted water supplies. Past illnesses and low social status take their toll on physical and mental health in older age (UNFPA, 1998).

Of course, any success in reducing these gender inequalities in health among the older age groups of poorer countries will then undoubtedly widen the presently narrow gender gap in life expectancies, and make them more akin to those of MDC populations where gender gaps arise more from inherent sex-differential mortality than from contrasting gender roles. It will also mean far more older women in the world than men, which may then instigate much more research towards overcoming the innate biological disadvantage of the male sex as far as longevity is concerned. It will also raise still further the problem of support for older women living alone, whose lot has often suffered from the decline and fragmentation of the geographically localised extended families and the growth of dispersed nuclear families. Most are widows.

4.9   Marriage and Widowhood

Marriage influences life expectancy. Although new types of relationships are evolving and the forms of marriage and age at marriage vary greatly around the world, its incidence varies much less, as it is still a widespread institution. In recent years the ideal of companionate marriage has spread, but there is no evidence of a major convergence to one 'modern' form of relationship (UNFPA, 1998: 35). Unfortunately, once again, in considering marriage data we have to make the usual caveats about unreliability and deficiency for most countries, so estimates have to be used. Moreover, responses to census questions on this topic may not be very accurate, as divorced and separated persons may be reported as single, married or widowed, and couples in consensual unions may be reported as married.

Despite changes in the institution of marriage, for women aged 50 (when all those likely to marry have already done so) its incidence averages about 96% world-wide, but the range is from near universality in most of Africa and Asia to 80–90% in much of the Caribbean, Latin America and some parts of Sub-Saharan Africa, where consensual unions are very common, and in some Catholic European countries such as Spain, Italy and Ireland, where traditions of spinsterhood still persist and act as a break on fertility (Noin, 1991: 64–5).

The sex-differential in the life expectancy of married persons is very much greater than that of single, widowed or divorced persons, women appearing to cope better than men with the non-married state (Retherford, 1975). Even in the shock of the first year of widowhood, when there is an excess mortality resulting partly from living conditions, widows fare better than widowers. Analysis of French civil registration data for 1969 to 1991 has shown that during this first critical year excess mortality is +80% for widowers and +60% for widows, and although excess mortality declines subsequently the data show that widows survive longer (Thierry, 1999).

The marital situations of older men and women are strongly contrasted. Most older women become widows, while most older men are married, many of them having remarried. This differential is very striking in both MDCs and LDCs alike. In most countries, married older men greatly outnumber older widowers, especially among the 65–74 age group but also among those aged 75 and over. Among men aged 60 and over the proportion of widowers is generally under 20%. In contrast, in most countries 40–60% of older women are widows, except in some European countries and Latin America where the percentage is 30–40, and in some LDCs (e.g. Bangladesh, Egypt, Kuwait and South Korea) where well over 60% of all older women are widows, in comparison with less than 15% of men of this age who are widowers. Moreover, in some LDCs, as for example Indonesia and South Korea, over 85% of all women aged 75 or more are widowed. In most MDCs (e.g. United Kingdom and Canada) the percentage is more like 65, but this rises with age, and the widows are supplemented by an increasing number of older divorced and separated women who now usually outnumber their male counterparts.

To give an indication of the scale of outnumbering, in the United States in 1997 there were 9.9 million widowed and divorced women aged 65 and over compared with only 2.9 million men, but while 42.4% of women aged 65–74 and 66.7% of those aged 75 and over were widowed or divorced the comparable figures for men were only 16.7% and 29.6%; and if the never married are added in there were 10.7 million unmarried women aged 65 and over compared with only 3.5 million unmarried men, a sex ratio of 31 (Eshleman, 2000: 448–50).

There are at least five times as many widows as widowers in a number of African and Asian countries: Algeria, Bangladesh, Botswana, Burkina Faso, Burundi, Cameroon, Egypt, Ivory Coast, Jordan, Mali, Morocco, Senegal, Tunisia and Zimbabwe (UNFPA, 1998: 58). Married older women are greatly and increasingly outnumbered by older widows, especially in the age groups 75 and over. An obvious fact is that the numbers of older widows are growing rapidly world-wide.

Several factors account for this profusion of older widows. First, as we have seen in the previous section, in most parts of the world women tend to live longer than men and differential life expectancy is generally increasing. But as life expectancies are rising rapidly, men and women will have a surviving spouse to a much greater age, even in LDCs. For example, while in 2000 about 52% of all South Korean women aged 65–69 were widows, by 2050 that percentage is likely to drop to 17.

The second reason is that in most societies more widowers remarry than widows, and that is particularly true for the elderly widowed. One fact is that most men are less able to cope domestically living alone and need 'looking after', women being the main carers, but another is that in most populations differential life expectancy ensures that older widows have less potential partners than older widowers, who have a widening choice. In MDCs during recent decades, the decline in marriage rates and the rises in the incidence of cohabitation, the age of marriage, the rate of divorce and the rate of remarriage, especially of men, have been major social changes, particularly marked in Northern and Western Europe, although the rate of remarriage tended to decline over the last two decades of the twentieth century partly because of increased cohabitation after divorce (Eshleman, 2000: 518). The United States has the highest remarriage rate in the world, over 40% of all marriages, but in the United Kingdom today one marriage in three is a remarriage of one or both partners. This is much more common than in LDCs, where religious traditions often impede remarriage, especially of women.

Thirdly, nearly everywhere in the world women usually marry men older than themselves, with a world average gender gap in marriage age of about 4 years, the average age being about 25.5 years for men and 21.5 for women. Reflecting local customs and traditions, the range of the average gender gap in marriage age by country is very wide, from about 1.1 years in Jamaica to 10.8 years in Guinea. In most MDCs the average gender gap in marriage age is only 2–3 years, but, as already mentioned, in many such countries the whole institution of marriage and its statistical incidence are being dramatically affected not only by the growing frequency of divorce but also by the recent rapid increase in the incidence of cohabitation and the various types of free and consensual unions. The latter helps to account for the narrow gender gap in marriage age in many parts of Latin America and the Caribbean, as well as two surprisingly contrasting countries with the world's highest average marriage ages, Sweden and Jamaica, revealing once more that the MDC/LDC dualism is not always demographically sharp. In these two countries, both bride and groom are on average 30 years old or more, the groom being 1–2 years older than the bride, but a corollary of this late marriage age is that they have some of the highest rates of births to unmarried women. Jamaica records the highest such rate in the world, 84% of all births, and Sweden's rate of 50% is only exceeded by El Salvador (67%) and Panama (75%), all in vivid contrast, for example, with only 1% of all births to unmarried women in Egypt, Japan and South Korea (Neft and Levine, 1997). In most LDCs, however, the gender gap in marriage age is characteristically much wider than in MDCs, and is usually 4–10 years. It is especially wide in those countries of Africa, South Asia and South West Asia where early marriage of teenage girls, so-called 'child marriage', persists. In the mid-1990s there were at least 24 countries where the average age at first marriage of the bride was less than 20 years, and in nearly half of these the average age is less than 18 years, all poor and mostly Muslim countries in either Sub-Saharan Africa (Guinea, Niger, Mali, Chad, Ethiopia, Burkina Faso, Malawi and Angola) or Asia (Yemen, Afghanistan and Nepal).

In *Yemen*, the average age at first marriage of a bride is as low as 15 years, perhaps the lowest in the world and nearly 8 years younger than the average age of the groom. Not surprisingly, it is currently the country with the highest fertility rate (7.6 children per woman), one of the highest maternal mortality rates (1400 deaths per 100,000 live births), and with one of the lowest female life expectancies at birth (only 52.4 years).

Happily, world-wide the marriage of teenage girls is gradually becoming less common, especially in cities and under the influence of the widespread increase in female education and employment, although it still prevails in isolated rural areas of many LDCs. But progress is uneven, and has sometimes been hindered by religious fundamentalism and the fact that the minimum legal age of marriage with parental consent is still in the low teens in many countries. The existence of considerable continental differences in the average gender gap in marriage age is one clear reflection of the persistently strong cultural variations in the status and autonomy of women, gender inequalities that do not change overnight (Hertrich and Locoh, 1999).

Obviously, widowhood or the loss of a long-term partner has a major impact on the incomes, lifestyles, households and housing of older women. In LDCs, widows are often illiterate and innumerate, have limited inheritance rights, few resources, savings or pensions, and in patriarchal societies they have often been unused to decision-making (UNFPA, 1998: 58). Widowhood brings an immediate loss of status, from a fairly low level anyway. The lot of widows has never been an easy one, even when they are young, and in some countries many have resorted to prostitution, particularly in those where polygamy is common (e.g. Ghana and other West African countries). Widowhood is a difficult status in most societies, whether characterised by nuclear or extended families, but it is especially difficult where the remarriage of widows is forbidden, as in Nepal, or as in other countries like India where it is regarded (at least by men) as unacceptable for widows with children to remarry (Pearson, 1987).

India exemplifies very well many of the problems of widowhood experienced by LDCs, as it has probably more widows at every age than in any other country. Although the incidence of widowhood has been declining over recent decades, largely because of general improvements in both male and female longevity, at the time of the 1991 census there were more than 33 million widows, a little above 8% of the total female population, 50% of all women aged over 50 years and nearly 80% of those aged 70 and over (Chen, 1998). A vast, vulnerable and neglected section of the Indian population, they suffer from above-average morbidity and mortality and constitute a real social problem that is not fully recognised. The main reasons for the profusion of widows are that marriage in India is nearly universal and husbands are on average 4–5 years older than their wives, but on the death of their husbands few wives of any age remarry, except young widows who have no children. It is shocking to note that there are still child widows in India, even 'virgin widows' whose marriage had not been consummated before the death of their husbands (Chen, 1998). Under Hindu tradition, women were regarded as symbols of purity and family honour, and widows who did not commit sati were enjoined not to remarry and were expected to follow a chaste, austere lifestyle that often involved harsh living conditions in the

Table 4.6 Sex ratios of the older population of Kerala, southern
India, by marital status, 1991

	60 +	70 +	80 +
Elderly	**87.2**	**82.9**	**80.5**
Married	201.2	278.6	328.9
Widowed	13.1	16.8	23.2

Source of data: Prakash, 1999: 55.

villages of their former husbands. In one sense, widowhood was a form of
birth control. Now the situation is improving. It is sometimes stated that
widow remarriage is prohibited in Hindu society, but that is really only
true for upper castes, most other castes allowing it although it is generally
uncommon. Some have even practised leviratic unions, whereby a widow
remarries her deceased husband's brother, a practice that has taken place
among peasant castes in Haryana when the demand for female labour and
fertility has been high.

In contrast to the high percentage of widows in India, in 1991 only about
2.5% of all Indian men were widowers, less than a third of the number of
widows, mainly because widowers are very much freer to remarry and indeed
by Hindu tradition they have been encouraged to do so. Consequently, there
is a much higher rate of remarriage among widowers than widows, so that
widowers constitute only a small minority of men even among older age
groups.

Inevitably in India, there are cultural and regional variations in the
incidence of widowhood, it being lower in most of the northern states than
it is in the south. This is largely because of a greater age differential at
marriage in the south, higher remarriage rates in the north and higher
mortality rates among northern widows (Chen, 1998). Kerala demonstrates
clearly the very low sex ratios of the older widowed population found in
southern India (Prakash, 1999), as seen in Table 4.6 (although once again
we recall that the Indian census expresses sex ratios differently as the number
of females per thousand males). However, the greater incidence of clan and
village exogamy in northern than in southern India means that on becoming
widows northern women are much more isolated than their southern
counterparts, and have less freedom to claim land ownership or to obtain
employment.

In the world as a whole, it has been estimated that more than 30% of all one-
person households have an older person, and that in many countries more than
half of all persons living alone are elderly (United Nations, 1993: 57). Of course,
in most parts of the world the percentage of widows living alone is much greater
than that of widowers, often twice as large. There is little doubt that their
increasing numbers will necessitate better support systems in the future. At

present in MDCs many widowed grannies are finding new roles as carers for grandchildren when parents are out at work, roles that are all the more important for one-parent households. But they experience an increasing amount of residential segregation, when perhaps integration is more desirable, and inevitably this means that they comprise the great majority of people living in residential, retirement and nursing homes, especially at advanced ages. This fact is most notable in large cities and especially in the many centres of retirement migration which also function as holiday resorts, such as the many towns around the coasts of Britain where wives who have migrated with their husbands at retirement normally outlive them by several years, thus lowering the sex ratios in resorts like Budleigh Salterton, Bognor Regis and Bournemouth. Older men, on the other hand, are often more numerous than older women in rural areas, and this is the case for MDCs and LDCs alike (US Bureau of Census, 1992), but it is often a reflection of differential migration, the women having migrated to the towns. This is the topic that we shall turn to now.

CHAPTER 5

MALE AND FEMALE MOBILITY

5.1 Shortage of Studies

People are nearly always on the move, but males and females do not move about in equal numbers. Primarily, that is because of behavioural differences in gender roles rather than biological differences in sex. Consequently, in this chapter we focus on mobility and gender.

Geographical mobility (quite different from social mobility) is nearly always differentiated by gender, but that differentiation varies greatly with the almost infinite diversity of human movements. The characteristics of the many different types of human mobility vary immensely over space and time: in cause, course, composition, consequence, duration, direction, distance, volume, rate of flow, organisation and relationship to political and administrative units. Consequently, so do the ratios of male to female movers. Women are now very roughly estimated by the United Nations to make up half of the world's migrant population, yet perhaps surprisingly until the 1990s there were only a few substantial studies of population movements differentiated by gender (e.g. Fawcett *et al.*, 1984) and few specifically about the mobility of women. Fortunately, that situation is being rectified rapidly, especially by a growing number of researchers undertaking micro-studies in the field (see Pedraza, 1991; Chant, 1992; Fairhurst *et al.*, 1997; Boyle and Halfacree, 1999; Hugo, 1999; Findley, 1999; Willis, 2000).

Unfortunately, data at the macro level about human mobility differentiated by gender are not always available. For many human movements (e.g. refugees, displaced persons) there are only crude estimates of the overall numbers for countries of source and destination, with no satisfactory disaggregation by gender or any other population characteristic. One reason for this deficiency is that in the past men have been regarded as the main movers, and women and families as secondary to that process, despite the fact they may have influenced it greatly and have been greatly affected by it. Also there is little doubt that men have dominated the short-term movements of workers, and as 'heads of household' they have been the main respondents to survey questionnaires about movements. Consequently, data collection has been biased against women.

It is now widely accepted that there is a great need for better age and sex data about mobility, and that the mobility of males and females should be differentiated in order to respond to their different needs and to understand the processes involved (United Nations, 1991). Nevertheless, progress in this direction is slower than desirable, and there is a good deal of evidence to suggest that women's experience of mobility is still affected by policies and rules that subtly treat women as subordinate within male-regulated societies (Koser and Lutz, 1998).

5.2 Increasing Female Mobility

Great geographical diversity occurs in the degree of differential mobility by gender, because gender roles, rights, status and employment differ strongly from society to society and from country to country, based largely on cultural traditions. The one certainty is that nowhere is there gender equality in mobility, only inequality. Furthermore, men and women do not move for the same reasons. In almost all societies men move further, more frequently and much more freely than women over a wider age range, but the level and types of mobility made by men and women that are considered appropriate in one society are often unacceptable in another. This is especially true for female mobility, which has long been largely controlled and directed by men. However, as we shall see, that situation is changing rapidly. During the second half of the twentieth century there have been immense socio-economic changes in women's overall status, age of marriage, level of education, amount of child-bearing and rate of labour-force participation, all of which have contributed to a great increase in their independence and liberty, as well as in the diversity of their movements, especially within MDCs. Women movers are also especially influenced by complex household strategies (including reproduction) which are as important as labour opportunities in explaining their mobility (Chant, 1992; Findley, 1999; Hugo, 1999).

The roles of women in the decision to move have long been underestimated (Morokvasic, 1984; Campani, 1995). Certainly, they are increasing and patriarchal attitudes are diminishing, but in addition there has been a great overall increase in female mobility, not only for family reunification but also because growing family fragmentation enables women to move more autonomously for employment (Koser and Lutz, 1998). Much of this has been associated with the massive growth and concentration of the secondary, tertiary and quaternary economic sectors in large and generally expanding urban centres. Initially in MDCs but latterly in many newly industrialising countries, tens of millions of

women, alone (unmarried, separated, divorced or widowed), with husbands/
partners or in family groups, have moved from the country into the towns,
seeking employment in a wide range of activities but especially as textile,
assembly, domestic, office, shop and entertainment workers, and this has greatly
increased the proportion of females in migration streams. Mercurial and widespread urbanisation associated with the huge growth of the service sector all
over the world during the second half of the twentieth century has been very
attractive to female migration and employment, and latterly more and more
educated women are finding jobs within the service sector in larger cities.
Women are also becoming much more vocal in family migration decision-
making, especially in households with two or more incomes, which tend to
have a restrictive effect on migratory moves because finding two or more jobs
at the same time is not easy. All the indications are that the twenty-first century
will bring further widespread changes to the status, roles and liberty of women,
so we should see many more modifications in gendered mobility.

5.3   Mobility, Migration and Circulation

The ever-changing complexity of types of mobility, influenced by manifold social,
economic, political and environmental changes as well as by the rapid evolution
of the different forms of transport, makes them extremely difficult to classify.
No single system of classification has been widely accepted, partly because new
types of mobility are emerging all the time and mobility is increasingly globalised.
Modern advanced societies have been characterised as experiencing *hypermobility*, which is closely correlated with the growth of electronic communication.
Adams (1999) notes that the average Briton in 1950 travelled about 5 miles a day,
whereas at the end of the century it was 28 miles and this was expected to double
by 2026, replacing old-fashioned geographical communities by aspatial communities of interest. Who fifty years ago would have envisaged the growth of mass
inter-continental movements of tourists from MDCs and of workers from LDCs?
Or the rapid rise in the numbers of refugees, particularly in many of the poorer
parts of the world? The diversity in the types of human movement is such that all
manner of classifications of human displacements have been devised (see e.g.
Bilsborrow *et al.*, 1984), but none is wholly satisfactory. This situation is not
helped by the inadequacy of much of the data and the unfortunate fact that
the terminology tends to vary by discipline and by country and is thus far from
being uniform and standardised. Broadly, conceptualisation of human mobility
involves consideration of four main dimensions: changes in location, residence,
activity space and time. Incorporating them all into any taxonomy results in a
complex system which inevitably does not gain wide public or even academic
acceptance.

The most widely but not universally accepted distinction is that between long-term geographical mobility of population, which is normally called migration, and short-term mobility, which is often known as circulation. Migrations are usually defined as the movement of individuals or groups to a permanent or semi-permanent change of residence, and for census definition they involve both the crossing of an administrative boundary and a time factor, usually one year. Circulation incorporates all those human movements not involving a permanent or long-lasting change of residence. Inevitably, a clear-cut distinction between the two categories is impossible; much depends on how permanent is permanent.

This dualism, like many others, is of course a gross simplification of reality, but it is useful for our purposes, because movements by gender are affected by whether they are temporary or permanent. We should recognise, however, that the term circulation is less commonly recognised by the general public than that of migration, and that some writers do not recognise circulation and apply the term migration to all the numerous forms of human mobility. In addition to this dualistic classification, the great variety of human movers is categorised by a host of more or less commonly used terms all capable of different definitions, such as nomads, semi-nomads, transhumants, hunter-gatherers, migrant labourers/workers, contract labourers, refugees, displaced persons, asylum seekers, invaders, indentured labourers, expatriates, repatriates, in-migrants, out-migrants, immigrants, emigrants, transmigrants, settlers, commuters, travellers and gypsies. The list is not exhaustive and none of these terms is wholly exclusive or discrete; all have blurred edges. Moreover, apart from the widely used terms in-migration and out-migration, immigration and emigration that are used respectively in relation to internal and external migration, the generic terms 'migrants' and 'migration' are qualified in the scientific literature by an increasing number of adjectives to describe more or less specific types: periodic, oscillating, relay, seasonal, temporary, circular, transfer, transit, return, step, forced, involuntary, voluntary, spontaneous, skilled, organised, state-supported, passive, autonomous, individual, family, clandestine, illegal, undocumented, retirement, rural-urban, rural-rural, urban-rural, urban-urban, intra-urban, interregional, internal, external, international and inter-continental. Even this extensive list of adjectives used in connection with migration is far from comprehensive, as new types of migration are constantly being identified, and once again authors may define these terms differently. Obviously, all these different types of human movement involve different numbers and ratios of males and females.

It almost goes without saying that the blurred distinction between migration and circulation can lead to considerable confusion. Migrants are often termed either permanent or temporary, with no clear-cut time threshold between the two categories. Moreover, circulation may often lead on to definitive migration, whether initially intended or not, as temporarily intended moves often become more permanent through marriage, cohabitation or economic factors such as the acquisition of a permanent job. A further complication is the fact that many people in rich and poor countries alike have more than one residence and move between their different locations, while others (e.g. nomads, travellers and gypsies) take their residence with them – they are all multi-locational. Rural-urban migrants often retain possession of their rural farms and residences long after migrating to cities, and move backwards and forwards thus combining rural and urban lives. The phenomenon of 'second homes', once confined to the wealthier people in society, has not only expanded greatly but become increasingly international, and has led to movements such as those practised by the so-called 'snowbirds' of Europe and North America, older people who escape the colder winters of the north to more southerly sunnier climes in the Mediterranean or the Caribbean.

While by definition circulation involves return movements, migration streams also generally have counter streams. This is a significant point in the context of gender because the long-term sex ratio of a particular population is less affected by the sex ratio of *gross migration* (the sum of the numbers of in-migrants and out-migrants, or of immigrants and emigrants if we are considering international migrations), than by the sex ratio of net migration (the balance between the amounts of in-migration and out-migration, or immigration and emigration). The ratio of net to gross migration varies greatly from one migration stream to another, as one stream may be definitive with no returns while another may be largely or even entirely reversed. When the return flows of migrants are strong, net migration may be only a tiny fraction of gross migration and the long-term impact upon the population and its sex ratio negligible. Obviously, the sex ratios of gross and net migrations may also differ substantially. So, as we shall see, it is no easy task to generalise about migrations and their relationships to gender.

While migration greatly affects the long-term sex ratio of a residential population, circulation has more effect on what is now increasingly termed the gender balance within society, the ever-changing relative numbers of men and women in workplaces, places of leisure, institutions, authorities and associations. As the status of women gradually improves, the long-standing lack of gender balance in social, economic and political organisations is a matter of considerable current concern in many countries, although more under attack in some than in others. In Britain, for example, the gender imbalance in government, Parliament and at higher levels in the professions has attracted particular attention and is being tackled under the heading of equal opportunities, but of course the imbalance is evident throughout society down to the level of club memberships and management committees – even the word 'management' has tended to exclude women. Equal opportunities legislation in many MDCs is having an impact on the balance and is affecting differential movements of men and women, but there is a long way to go to achieve equality. It is therefore interesting to compare and contrast the respective selectivities of migration and circulation by gender, and how they influence directly and indirectly the sex ratios of populations.

5.4 Some Generalisations about Migration and Gender

Migrants rarely migrate entirely individually, without involving others, except in the case of young men over the short term. Women have been less likely to migrate autonomously, independently or individually, and have moved much more in association with husbands, and with families or households in which their roles are variously specified. However, family/household migration does not always involve the movement of a complete family/household unit at a specific time, but may involve sequential moves, the husband often moving first followed later by other members of the family/household. Communities are also involved, engendering links and networks between source and destination, facilitating the flows forwards and backwards of migrants, goods, information and remittances (Chant, 1992: 16–7).

As far as distance of migrations is concerned, there is an inevitable tendency for men to predominate in long-distance migrations and for women to be more prominent in short-distance migrations especially within countries, but once again this not a rigid rule, because in some parts of the developing world, as in many but not all countries of Sub-Saharan Africa, male migrants are more numerous over all migration distances. Traditionally, women have had much more confined activity spaces, being more confined to hearth, home and locality than men. Cultural constraints, such as the custom of keeping women in purdah or seclusion, have been strong in patriarchal Muslim and Hindu societies, but in most societies women have had much less freedom to undertake long-distance migrations to relatively unknown destinations unless accompanied. Of course, there have been exceptions, among whom were the remarkable group of nineteenth century European women explorers of Africa and the Middle East.

Migrations are very gender selective, their population compositions rarely matching those of the populations at either source or destination, except of course on unusual occasions when a whole population is forced to migrate involuntarily in an undifferentiated way. Because of the restraining influence of home and property ownership, such migrations tend to be only activated by natural disasters (e.g. earthquakes, volcanic eruptions, floods, droughts) or major human catastrophes (e.g. conflicts, wars, famines), and then often only temporarily (Clarke *et al.*, 1989). It follows that in more normal circumstances migrations are constantly altering the sex ratios of residential populations.

In any particular locality the frequency of migratory moves per annum tends to be greater than the frequency of either births or deaths, so migrations tend to have a much greater effect on sex ratios at local level than either births or deaths. Obviously, their numerical significance to sex ratios of populations diminishes among larger populations in larger areal units, such as those at national and continental level, because the larger the areal unit of population the more migrations are contained internally within it and the smaller the role played by external migrations in overall population change. Until we reach the days

when numerous space travellers will be leaving the earth to go off to other parts
of the universe, external migrations will have no influence at all on the sex ratio
of the global population.

Unlike birth and death, a migration is a process, not a finite, clearly defined
event that is relatively easy to measure. It is a physical and social transition
(Pooley and Turnbull, 1998) affecting populations and environments at both
source and destination. Yet when considering overall changes taking place in
populations, migration is temporally and spatially a much more irregular, spasmodic and less continuous demographic phenomenon than either human fertility
or mortality. Because migrations are also extremely diverse, their degree of
selectivity varies greatly as well; some migrations are mostly male, some mostly
female, some are more balanced. And the selectivity of most migrations changes
a great deal over time. Migrations are also less inevitable than deaths and less
controllable than births.

Migrations can be influenced greatly by government policies but they are
rarely physically controlled for long, despite strong attempts to do so in author-
itarian states such as in China. Boundaries have a constraining effect on migrations, and are to a greater or lesser extent demographic divides. Migrations may
be much more easily controlled along national boundaries than along internal
boundaries, but many geometric and undemarcated national boundaries, as over
much of the heart of the Sahara, are extremely difficult to patrol and control
effectively, while others, such as those within the European Union, are deliber-
ately being made much more open and passable as a result of inter-governmental
agreements and economic collaboration.

Migration is not entirely separable from fertility and mortality from a demographic viewpoint, as births and deaths take place before, during and after
migrations. Many migrant streams consist primarily of young adults in the
reproductive age groups, and if the migrants move as families they may have
striking effects upon the fertility of the host country. This is the case in the
United Kingdom, where the sex ratios of immigrants have usually been male-
dominated but a notable percentage of all live births has been to mothers born
overseas; over a fifth in many large cities like London, with a consequent considerable impact upon population growth. It is of course a major factor in the
growth of the multi-ethnicity of West European cities and countries, exemplified
visibly by the ethnic composition of their sports teams, as for example France's
successful squad of World Cup footballers in 1998.

We have mentioned that traditionally men have been much more migratory
than women, migrating mainly to find work and that women have either accompanied them or followed on later, adopting the role often known as 'passive
migrants'. Many of the movements of women have either been *en famille* or
associational, greatly influenced by the movements of male members of their
families whether they accompanied them or not. Women left behind when men
have migrated have often been extremely vulnerable. Unfortunately, this was not

reflected in many of the early studies of migration, which ignored the gender composition of migrants and in particular the migration of women, partly because it was seen to be so interrelated with that of men (Hoerder and Moch, 1996: 10). Fortunately, that deficiency is being rectified following the dramatic changes in the status of women during the second half of the twentieth century and the consequent increases in their migration.

5.5   Gender Changes in the Evolution of Migration Streams

Selectivity by gender varies during the evolution of a migration stream. In the early stages of most migration streams, men have tended to outnumber women. In the past, some migrations were very male-dominated in the early stages, the migration of women and children being seen as followers dependent upon the movements of men.

For instance, the early demographic histories of the former British colonies of **Singapore** and **Hong Kong** were dominated by immigration of men and their sex ratios reflected this. **Singapore** had less than 200 people when it was purchased by Sir Stamford Raffles in 1819, but its population grew largely through immigration from China and India of poor male plantation workers who eventually turned to commerce, its population rising to 227,000 by 1901 and to 558,000 by 1931, of whom 75% were Chinese. During all this time the sex ratio was very imbalanced, and was roughly 310 for most of the second half of the nineteenth century. Then it declined slowly until the 1920s and 1930s when quite large numbers of Chinese women arrived to restore the gender balance a little, partly by boosting the birth rate.

A rather similar situation occurred in **Hong Kong**, which had 'over 12,000' people when it was ceded to the United Kingdom in 1842, but that small population grew rapidly mostly through the arrival of Chinese merchants, labourers and refugees, reaching a total of 275,000 and a peak sex ratio of 265 in 1901, and subsequently rising to a total of 821,000 with a much lower sex ratio of 135 in 1931 as the immigrant population became more settled.

Of course, much has happened since then in both Singapore and Hong Kong, including the Japanese invasions during the Second World War and rapid post-war population and economic growth, so that their demographies are now very different. Natural increase now plays a more important role in influencing the sex ratios of both Singapore and Hong Kong, but both still have more males than females. Independent Singapore's population in the mid-1990s had risen to 3.5 million with a much more balanced sex ratio of 103, while the colony of Hong Kong's had surged

to 6.3 million with a sex ratio of about 105. Hong Kong's recent incorporation within China will undoubtedly have major demographic effects.

The early overseas migrations of Europeans to settle in colonial dependencies in
the Americas, Africa and Australasia were also heavily male-dominated, though
the proportion of women was greater among the migrants from North and West
Europe (especially Ireland) than among those from South and East Europe. The
proportion of female migrants usually increased as wives and families joined the
expanding settlements, particularly during the twentieth century.

Portugal's present population structure, with one of the lowest sex ratios in
Western Europe (93 in 1997), reflects the prolonged effect of large-scale
emigration as a safety valve in a country where until recently natural
increase has long oustripped economic growth, especially in densely peopled
northern Portugal where regional sex ratios are still below 90. In the nineteenth century and first half of the twentieth century, Brazil was the main
destination for emigrants, the majority of whom were men of peasant
origin. Between 1891 and 1960 over 1.44 million emigrants went to settle
in Brazil, secondary destinations being Argentina, the United States and
Europe. In the 1960s, emigration switched to European destinations, and
there was a net loss of about a million migrants especially to France, but
this movement was from all parts of Portugal, was less male-dominated and
was less permanent, many migrants returning home for holiday visits.
Nevertheless, when emigration to other European countries reached a
peak in 1970, the national sex ratio was only 90.2, although the precise
impact of sex-differential migration is difficult to estimate (Dewdney and
White, 1986). Subsequently, emigration gradually declined and diversified,
the movement to Brazil dying out and more emigrants going to the United
States and Canada. The demographic and economic situations have also
been transformed following the coup of 25 April 1974, by the returns of
hundreds of thousands of *retornados* from the decolonised the African
countries of Angola and Mozambique and of *regressados* from Europe,
by the benevolent effects of membership of the European Union, and by
exceptionally low population fertility which has reduced natural increase to
below zero and reduced also the pressure to emigrate.

In contrast, *New Zealand* has long been a country of destination for
emigrants, and until the 1970s its population nearly always contained
more males than females. Because men greatly outnumbered women
among the early immigrants, the sex ratios were very high in the nineteenth
century, when the population was small. In 1867, when the population was
just under 220,000, the sex ratio was 151, i.e. males accounted for well over
two-thirds of the total, and in the 15–64 age group it was much higher still
at 190. Even the Maori population, then numbering about 50,000, was also

male-dominant with a sex ratio of about 130. A better balance of the sexes in New Zealand was only achieved when there were more female immigrants and when natural increase began to challenge immigration as the main cause of population growth (Neville, 1979). So by 1906, when there were 936,000 inhabitants, the sex ratio had fallen appreciably to 113, and it was only 115 for the 15–64 age group. By 1936, when the total population was 1,574,000, it had dropped much further to 103, which was also the sex ratio of the 15–64 age group. Thereafter, although immigration was still male-dominant its net volume was small and therefore it played a limited role in influencing the overall sex ratio, which has been below 100 since 1971 and is now only 98.

Another factor in European overseas migration was that legislation, American law in particular, encouraged the reunion of families. Some women from North and West Europe, where normally marriage was unusually late, were also migrating independently for marriage overseas or to escape from the prospect of a local marriage that would have tied them to their home village. They were also migrating in very large numbers to enter domestic service in European cities or overseas.

Thus, the percentage of female migrants to the **United States** rose from annual averages of between 30 and 45% during the decades between 1820 and 1899 to averages of between 44 and 61% during the decades between 1920 and 1979 (Gabaccia, 1996:91). Today, the economic incentive is less and the social incentive greater, with the bulk of the immigrants into the United States going to join a family rather than to work. The overall effect has been that the male-dominant early nineteenth century migrations were replaced by much more balanced migration streams during the twentieth century. Another factor influencing the sex ratios of migrants is that men were more frequent returnees. Although men left homes in Europe for migration to the United States more often than women, they also returned more often. Once they had arrived in the States, women tended to stay and "returned less often than men regardless of the overall migration rate for the (national) group, its sex ratio, or whether they were married or single" (Jackson and Moch, 1996: 77). The gender balances of migrants and returnees were also greatly affected by the welcome in the receiving country and the ease or difficulty of assimilation, as well as the strength of the push factor at source. Thus Irish and Jewish women settled in more easily and were more inclined to stay in the States than women of most other nationalities.

On the other hand, it should not be thought that there is a rule that men are always more frequent returnees, because (as for so many demographic phenomena) there is considerable evidence to the contrary. In many LDCs, such as Peru, Philippines and Thailand, women migrants attach greater importance than men to retaining family ties with their homelands, and try more than men to revisit their home villages (Chant, 1992: 17).

5.6   Political Factors in Gendered Migration

The intentions of migrants about staying away from their place of origin are obviously critical to the gender composition of migration streams, but much also depends on the strength and nature of push factors at origin, of pull factors at destination and of the numerous intervening obstacles, such as distance, political boundaries, language, culture, customs and costs. The sex ratio of migrants is also affected by the extent to which the migration is voluntary or involuntary. Voluntary migration is generally gender selective, whether it is that of skilled or professional workers attracted by new employment elsewhere, sometimes called a 'brain drain', or the migrations to former colonial territories. Involuntary or forced migration, on the other hand, is much less gender selective, as seen in the forced removals of whole populations in South Africa under *apartheid*, the 'ethnic cleansing' practised in the 1990s in various parts of the former Federal Republic of Yugoslavia, the flights of undifferentiated masses of political refugees, expellees and internally displaced people (IDPs) escaping from or driven out by political regimes and conflicts, and the so-called 'economic refugees' forced out by famine, drought or other natural disasters. Catastrophes, either natural or human, do not encourage selectivity of migrations, or selective data about them, whether they cross political boundaries or not. Even today, published data about international movements of the tens of millions of current refugees and asylum seekers are rarely differentiated (Kraly, 1997), and nor are the similar numbers of internally displaced people, estimated at 23 million in 1997–8 (Hampton, 1998). Refugees and internally displaced people often flee too quickly and are too disorganised to be easily counted, and their numbers change daily. Refugees cross boundaries at unrecognised points where police controls do not exist, and internally displaced people cross no controlled boundaries at all, so it is not surprising that much of the published data about these movements are merely crude estimates that are undifferentiated by gender.

> Political migrations have transformed the demographies of some states, and the Middle East region, which has been so long affected by economic and political turbulence, provides an obvious example in ***Jordan*** whose population multiplied eleven times between the first Arab-Israeli conflict of 1948 and its 1994 census when the total reached 4.1 million. Apart from a few micro-states, this was the fastest population growth rate in the world. It was brought about partly by rapid natural increase but mainly

by migration, particularly the major influxes of Palestinian and to a lesser extent Lebanese refugees as a result of Arab-Israeli wars, but supplemented in the 1990s by the return of over 200,000 workers and their families from the Gulf States at the time of the Gulf War. Jordan has been a stable refuge from political turmoil in the Middle East and has given nationality to large numbers of these refugees. As refugees they were not selected by gender, and thus the sex ratio of the 3.8 million in the present Jordanian population is not unusually high (105.3 in 1994) for a Middle Eastern country. In contrast, that of the 0.3 million foreigners in Jordan, mostly workers of diverse international origin, was very high (181.7), and among the younger adults the sex ratios were even higher (e.g. 354.1 among the 25–29 year-olds).

Political policies and controls have an obvious influence on the gender selectivity of migrations. It is the reason why so few Chinese women were admitted into the United States during the nineteenth century, and why for example many Western countries and Middle Eastern oil-rich countries have from time to time restricted the entry of the wives and families of male migrant workers who they wanted to exclude as permanent immigrants, especially those who have entered as contract workers, for fear of building up large foreign populations. Such controls have become a major contentious ethnic issue in the immigration policies of many countries, but of course much less so as far as emigration is concerned.

As evidence that international migrations are difficult to control, there are many millions of undocumented migrants who cross international boundaries illegally or overstay their permitted entries in an unauthorised, clandestine or surreptitious manner for political or economic reasons. In some countries their presence is tolerated as long as their labour is needed and the political relationships with their country of origin are friendly, but that tolerance tends to disappear when there is a threat to local employment, when demands upon social services become excessive or when the migrants get involved in other illegal activities. Inevitably, statistics of these illegal migrants tend to be largely 'guesstimates' undifferentiated by gender. Certainly the majority of them are men, although the globalisation of the sex industry has meant that there are now many more undocumented women migrants than formerly, focusing on large cities and on countries where that industry has thrived. For example, recent reports suggest that women from Eastern Europe have been flooding into the cities of Western Europe for this purpose.

5.7 Gendered Migration and Employment

Most migrants have employment in mind. Contrasting economic conditions, particularly spatial differences of employment opportunities in both supply and demand areas, at source and destination, greatly encourage gender selectivity of migrations, and neoclassical theory has emphasised the economic rationality of male and female migrants in response to these regional differences in economic opportunities (e.g. Thadani and Todaro, 1979).

Among traditional rural subsistence societies, the primary source areas of many migrants in the past, the migration of men to work elsewhere has enabled rural households to cope with the seasonal, annual and periodic fluctuations of farming, but it has had mixed socio-economic consequences; on the one hand increasing the economic roles of women, causing labour shortages and reducing local environmental care, but on the other improving food security and encouraging diversification through remittances.

It has been suggested that the migrations of women in such rural societies have been greatly influenced by their roles in food production and by the way that farming is organised (Boserup, 1970; Skeldon, 1990). When women are heavily involved in agriculture, as in many 'female farming' societies in Sub-Saharan Africa and in South Asia where they make up more than half of the agricultural workforce, they have been much less likely to migrate than men, so female migrants are greatly outnumbered by men, especially in long-distance migrations (Momsen and Townsend, 1987). In striking contrast, in 'male farming' systems where women play only a small role in agriculture, as in most Latin American countries particularly where agriculture has been capitalised and more mechanised, women are usually much more migratory, leaving the countryside to find work in the cities (Brydon and Chant, 1989; Chant, 1992; De Oliveira, 1991; Findley, 1999). However, it almost goes without saying that farming systems are not always very clearly dualised as either male-dominated or female-dominated. Women often play important roles in 'male farming' areas, and vice-versa. There are also some intensive farming systems that involve both men and women alike, such as those in the densely populated rice farming deltas of South East Asia, with consequent effects upon the gender selectivity of migrations. So once again this dualism should be treated only as a broad generalisation, with many exceptions.

Women are also prone to leave the harsher rural environments where job opportunities are few. Consequently, they often quit the mountains and moorlands, the deserts and the cold northern wastes.

In the North West Arctic region of **Alaska**, for example, Canadian Inuit women leave the rural areas because little work is available for them there, while the men are employed in mineral extraction and the oil industry. Consequently, in the early 1990s the sex ratio for 15–39 year-olds was 113 in the region as a whole, 132 in the villages and only 83 in the city of Anchorage. Hamilton and Seyfrit (1993) have furthermore pointed out that migration has a central role in facilitating gender differences in Inuit acculturation.

Employment opportunities for men and women in cities have also varied greatly over time. For example, until the eighteenth century most West European cities (the exceptions being religious, university or military towns) generally contained more females than males, a reflection of the long-term surplus of women, many of them single or widowed women from rural backgrounds working for a living as domestics (Fauve-Chamoux, 1998). Subsequently in the nineteenth century, the situation changed substantially with the huge growth in primary and secondary sector demand for male labour in mines and heavy industries, which was the major cause of rural-urban migration. Gradually that has changed again during the twentieth century with widespread industrial restructuring and the massive growth of the service sector in both MDCs and LDCs alike.

Employment opportunities for women have increased enormously in lighter industries and in innumerable service occupations. A structural approach to gendered migration emphasises how opportunities have increased with the segmentation of the labour market, which means that female migrants respond particularly to specific sectoral imbalances in the service sector and the informal economy rather than to overall imbalances in the labour market (e.g. Bennholdt-Thompson, 1984; Campani, 1995: 548).

It has been argued by Gordon (1995) that geographical variations in male and female labour migration in **Great Britain** are closely related to labour market segmentation, in particular the influence of organisation and power, distinguishing between different types of migrants:

- *sponsored migrants*, who work for the same company before and after the migration, or migrants receiving financial assistance for a migratory move;
- *unsponsored migrants*, who move speculatively or who are contracted but not sponsored by the employer;
- *port-of-entry migrants*, who move from full-time education into primary sector jobs; and
- *dependent migrants*, who are economically active females whose husbands' moves are job-related.

The 1988–89 British Labour Force Survey revealed that job-related movements by women were 40% less than those for men, largely because of less job-related moves for married women and because sponsored women migrants were only about half as numerous as men, indicating and indeed confirming the fact that women migrants experience discrimination. For many reasons, including better nursery places, a more feminist climate and better public transport, women migrants have also focused much more on London and the south-east of England than male migrants, who have dispersed more about the country (Boyle and Halfacree, 1995).

Unfortunately, sex discrimination in the labour market is still widespread, especially for women in ethnic minorities; women continue to find difficulties in achieving full-time employment (part-time employment is often associated with two-income households) and in attaining higher hierarchical levels of employment. So migrations of women are still impeded to a greater or lesser extent by the labour market, though the nature of that market varies considerably with the culture and economy of the society in question.

In general, women have been entering the global workforce in steadily increasing numbers, so that by 1995 they were estimated to account for 40% of the total, the growth being most rapid in the more industrialised countries (DeGraff and Anker, 1999). However, their share of the workforce ranges widely from country to country, from about 8% in Saudi Arabia to 50% in Slovenia, being lowest in many of the Muslim countries of the Middle East, South Asia and Africa and highest in a number of former communist countries in Eastern Europe (Neft and Levine, 1997). The contrasts are sharp. While in Afghanistan under Taliban rule women's share of the workforce has recently collapsed abruptly, in Britain it has risen rapidly to reach about 44% by the mid-1990s, and as in many other European countries more women are gaining jobs than men and less are losing them.

While employment opportunities have evolved differentially in economic and cultural regions, so has the selective migration of men and women. On the whole, young women mostly under the age of 20 migrate much more autonomously for education and the income-earning opportunities available in service industries and in labour-intensive light industries (sometimes called 'feminised') in Latin American and South East Asian cities than they do in South Asia, the Middle East and Tropical Africa, where the opportunities for employment of women in cities are less. Their lesser migration also results from the smaller numbers of single women (unmarried, separated, widowed and divorced), the lower average age of marriage of women and their more numerous children, as well as the prevalence of strong patriarchal control (Gugler, 1997).

5.8   Cultural and Social Factors in Gendered Migration

In addition to the neoclassical and structural economic explanations of gendered migration examined in the previous section, there is a more behavioural approach that takes into consideration the cultural constraints and the increasing social networks and institutions involved in migration (Caplan, 1985; Hugo, 1999).

As mentioned in Chapter 2, contrasts in selective migration are reflected in the urban sex ratios of the contrasting cultures of continental regions, those of cities in Latin America and to a lesser extent South East Asia being much lower than those of South and South West Asia and most of Sub-Saharan Africa. The urban sex ratios of selected countries shown in Table 2.5 gave some indication of these cultural and regional contrasts, but the situation is ever-changing. For example, in many Asian countries there has been a reduction in infant and child mortality followed by a decline in fertility that has led to a population boom and a 'youth bulge', so in an effort to reduce population growth rates their governments have encouraged young people, especially girls, to stay longer in school and to marry later. This meant that between 1950 and 1990 the percentage of women aged 15–24 remaining single and out-of-school rose in every country save Hong Kong, Japan, Taiwan, Thailand and the Philippines. In some countries this process has been accompanied by increased labour-force participation rates for young women, as for instance in Indonesia, Malaysia and Singapore. Although the latter increases are only a feature of those Asian countries where economic development and cultural conditions have encouraged more female employment, there are many indications of future increases in the rural-urban migration of women and thus further lowering of urban sex ratios.

Gugler (1997) proposes a hypothesis of gender transition in rural-urban migration for LDCs, leading to increased female participation in net rural-urban migration, but the increase in female migration into towns is no new phenomenon to MDCs. Well over a hundred years ago, E.G. Ravenstein (1885) in his classic paper on 'The Laws of Migration' noted that women outnumbered men in rural-urban migrations in Europe during the nineteenth century.

He also pointed out that in ***Britain*** a change to a female preponderance in internal migrations took place during the second half of the nineteenth century:

"Woman is a greater migrant than man. This may surprise those who associate women with domestic life, but the figures of the census clearly prove it. Nor do women migrate merely from the rural districts into the towns in search of domestic service, for they migrate quite as frequently into certain manufacturing districts, and the workshop is a formidable rival of the kitchen and the scullery" (Ravenstein, 1885:196).

Of course, Britain was ahead of other countries in industrialisation and urbanisation, and the change was later elsewhere. Generally the age profile of male and female migrants has been similar in Britain, although at most ages the migration rates of males are now higher than those of females, except among younger adults when the greater propensity of women to marry younger than men and to move from their parental home to their marital or cohabitation home has raised their migration rates above those of men (Devis and Southworth, 1984).

Life courses and events have always affected migrations, which reflect considerable cultural differences (Boyle, Halfacree and Robinson, 1998: 234). Marriage has been the most significant event. Migrations for marriage, by the husband or the wife or both, but generally the wife, have been a traditional feature of many societies, affecting their sex ratios according to their religious, ethnic and local customs. In India, for example, half of all female rural-urban migrants relocate as a result of marriage. Consequently, although female migration for employment reasons in India is generally limited, intra-state and intra-rural migration is heavily dominated by women, largely because of local moves for exogamous marriage in accordance with Hindu customs. In many Indian districts well over half of the women were born outside of the village where they live. Similarly in Japan, village exogamy prevails, with women moving to the male line, so that the gender ratios of short-distance moves are much lower than those of the male-dominated, employment-related, long-distance migrations (Skeldon, 1990: 118). The practice of exogamous marriage also occurs in much of Sub-Saharan Africa, with consequent effects upon the volume of female migration, but the complex plethora of societies in that region, with varied types of conjugal union (free, consensual, customary, formal marriage) and a high frequency of polygamous unions, tends to complicate the analysis of marriage migrations and deters simple generalisations. It is also complicated by the widespread practice of many young African wives returning temporarily to their mothers' homes for the birth of their child and for infant care until weaning, which in some West African populations has meant being away from their husbands for as long as two to three years.

In their study of female marriage migration in **China**, Fan and Huang (1999) have highlighted that marriage does not merely motivate migration but is also a strategy to achieve migration. In patrilocal rural China, where gender inequality still persists despite Maoist policies, daughters have traditionally left the household for arranged marriages locally, and consequently there has been little incentive for parents to invest in their education, the main return being a large brideprice at the time of marriage. Women are now now becoming more active in their own geographical and upward social mobility, and many are now moving for marriage much further away. Evidence from the 1990 census revealed that marriage was the reason for 28.2% and 28.9% of intraprovincial and interprovincial female migration respectively and was the leading cause of both. Facilitated by agents, long-distance marriage migration to selected regions experiencing economic growth, often over thousands of miles away, is a new phenomenon, so much so that south-western China (the provinces of Yunnan, Guizhou, Sichuan and Guangxi) has become known as the 'cradle of the bride'.

Marriage as a strategy for migration has also no doubt been a factor encouraging Russian women to leave Murmansk and Archangel, decaying and declining cities of north-western **Russia**, to cross the border into the sparsely peopled county of Finnmark in northern Norway, its richer neighbour where the sex ratio is high because so many Norwegian women have forsaken the rigours of arctic life for the blandishments and opportunities of Oslo.

Marriage migrations are just one example of the fact that gender selectivity of migrations is considerably affected by the cultural heritage of populations, whose varied household strategies reflect the diversity of division of labour and power within the household (Wood, 1981). Some populations have been much more territorially tethered and less migratory than others. In some cultures, female migration has been severely inhibited except for marriage, and women have been largely confined to the household; in others, women have had much greater autonomy and have been much more free to move autonomously. There are striking contrasts, for example, between the cultural constraints upon any long-distance migration by Middle Eastern and Japanese women and the much greater freedom to move experienced by many West African and North American women. But the picture is constantly changing. With the increasing speed and efficiency of many forms of transportation and with the widespread though not universal improvements in the status of women, the numbers of female migrants are increasing in many parts of the developed and developing world alike.

In many ways, the considerable retirement migration experienced in some MDCs, whereby retirees have moved to seaside resorts and holiday locations at home and abroad in order to escape from dreary climates and less salubrious industrial cities, may be regarded as partly a cultural phenomenon. Although it has been widespread in the West, it is rare in Japan. Such migration was especially common within Britain in the decades after the Second World War when retirees moved to holiday resorts and the countryside, but with the development of package holidays in sunnier climates it has since been extended to Mediterranean countries (e.g. Spain, Cyprus, Malta), the Caribbean and Florida. It led to a small peak of migration for men at 65–66 in the United Kingdom and 66–9 in the United States, but this was not clearly matched in the life courses of women, partly because they marry older men and retire earlier. Although retirement migration is usually of couples, differential mortality tends to have a selective effect through the earlier deaths of elderly husbands and the consequent isolation of elderly widows, and is thus the major cause of the low sex ratios common in the seaside resorts along the south coast of England. Perhaps growing awareness of the possibility of an unfortunate result of retirement migration is one reason for its declining attraction within Britain, many retirees now preferring to go on cruises, to take to numerous holidays in sunnier climes, or to buy second homes at home or abroad rather than to sell their main home and make a definitive retirement migration.

However, there are clear differences in the migrations of older men and women, especially after they are widowed, and the reasons are complex, resulting from various differences occurring in early and late old age: in income, health, availability of care, the likelihood of remarriage, and the ability to live alone (Warnes, 1999).

5.9   Circulation and Gender

There are almost innumerable forms of transient, temporary and repetitive circulation, including, for example, the seasonal movements of harvesters, pastoralists, catering workers and retirees, the periodic movements of traders, labourers, tourists and students, the intermittent travels of businessmen, politicians and scholars, and the daily or weekly journeys to work, shop, school, church or for leisure activities. Many of these moves are taking very much less time than formerly or involve more frequent trips, and all tend to be more gender-selective than permanent migrations.

   Of course, the increasing ability to travel huge distances in a short time means that nowadays even more movements are circulatory rather than migratory, that circulation accounts for an increasing proportion of human mobility, and that circulatory movements precede many migrations. Circulation has increased phenomenally during the twentieth century with the massive technological improvements in transport, notably in road and air travel, and with the equally massive changes in employment and workplaces, all greatly expanding people's activity spaces. The result is growing hypermobility (Adams, 1999). Circulation is no longer just local or national, but has become a global phenomenon as businessmen and women, tourists, backpackers, students and workers of all descriptions travel around the world. Activity spaces which were once regional or national are now continental or global. Moves that once would have taken months of travel and led to years of displacement are now reduced to short-term trips taking less than a day each way and perhaps an absence of a few days or a week. All have affected the balance of male and female circulation.

   Changes in social structures, notably the declines in family and household size in MDCs, have also brought about highly significant effects upon gendered circulation. For example, in many West European countries, low population fertility, rising numbers of small households, increasing female labour force participation rates and the spread of flexible employment patterns have meant a considerable increase in the number and proportion of dual career households (Green, 1995). Moreover, the increasing complexity of working and domestic lives has led to longer distance commuting as a substitute for migration, with members of the household going off in all directions to work (Green *et al.*, 1999).

   Selectivity by gender applies even more to circulation than to migration. Men usually outnumber women in circulatory moves and travel longer distances, because of the many social constraints upon the movement of women at source and their occupations at destination. Of course, the long-term impact on sex ratios is limited, because people are generally moving more or less briefly from a home base for a specific purpose that does not necessarily mean a change of residence or way of life.

In *Britain*, and most other countries, men usually travel further to and from work than women. The distances travelled by both men and women are increasing, especially for men, but the travel times for both remained more or less static during the twentieth century (Pooley and Turnbull, 1999). Those for women are generally at least as long as for men, because men have had faster mean journey speeds, having had access to more independent and private forms of transport than women, who have had to rely more on slower public transport. As women also account for a large proportion of part-time workers, the slower forms of transport obviously have had a profound effect upon their lifestyles particularly in the reproductive age-groups.

It has been mentioned already that short-term moves may well lead to long-term migration. Thus, the moves of numerous young Irish women to work as domestic servants to Britain during the nineteenth century, which reflected the marked contrasts in employment possibilities between famine-wracked rural Ireland and the newly industrialising towns of Britain, helped to create the large population of Irish origin now living in Britain and the persistence of male preponderance in rural Ireland. Such moves have been replicated in recent decades by much longer movements by large numbers of women workers from Southern to Northern Europe, and by even longer moves of women from the Philippines to work in Asia, Europe and the Middle East. In all these cases, many of these women workers intended to stay only a short time but ended up by living in their country of destination or moving on to another country. What started as temporary migration or circulation became permanent migration.

The Philippines have been a source of millions of overseas workers, a movement which accelerated following the rise in its unemployment rates during the 1980s. They are now said to go to more than 175 countries, an example of the staggering diffusion of modern workers and the globalisation of employment (Neft and Levine, 1997: 387–9), which brings in about US\$3 billion per annum in the form of remittances. Unusually for overseas workers, probably 65% are women (Filipinas), although the gender balance varies greatly according to the country destination, being much higher for instance among Filipino workers in Japan, Taiwan, Malaysia and Singapore than in more male-dominated Middle Eastern countries such as Saudi Arabia. Filipinas go overseas in order to work in all the traditional types of service employment, mainly as domestic servants, hotel employees, waitresses and nurses, as well as entertainers and sex workers. The latter specialism has long plagued the Philippines, having gained impetus with the stationing of American troops over many decades especially during the Second World War and the Vietnam War, but it has now become an export industry. Many Filipinas have even become 'mail order brides' for European, North American and Japanese men. Unfortunately, Filipina workers overseas, many of whom are undocumented, have often suffered from low wages as well as some lamentable experiences of violence and frequent sexual abuse. Retaliation by them has culminated in some much publicised murder cases in Japan, Singapore and the United Arab Emirates.

Unfortunately, the Philippines are far from being alone in witnessing the rise of the international sex industry. In Asia it has attracted and inveigled hundreds of thousands of Thai, Burmese, Chinese, Indian, Nepalese, Indonesian and Philippine women to leave their villages and to travel to large cities like Bombay or Bangkok, where it is highly developed (Matsui, 1999; Hugo, 1999). It is also massive in the mega-cities of South America, like Sao Paulo and Rio de Janeiro, and in many European cities, especially with the increasing mobility of population and the surge of international tourism. Few major cities in the world are exempt from migrants to the industry, and inevitably, many unfortunates have been left with HIV and AIDS.

Overseas workers usually send home remittances, but on the whole women overseas workers send home more remittances than the men (Curson, 1981). The failure by many men to send home regular remittances has meant that many women who have been left at home have had to fend for themselves with inter-mittent remittances or with none at all, as well as facing the possibility of desertion and divorce.

Lesotho, a small land-locked country of 30,300 sq. km. and about 2.2 million people entirely surrounded by South Africa, is an example of a country which has become heavily dependent upon the remittances sent home by absentees, mostly men who go to work in the mines of South Africa. The number of absentee workers has been such that the sex ratio of the *de facto* or resident population of Lesotho (81 at the 1986 census, but it has been much lower when absentees were even more numerous) has been substantially lower than that of the *de jure* population (93 in 1986) which includes those temporarily outside the country. Like many other small African so-called 'remittance societies' (e.g. Swaziland and Botswana), Lesotho's absentee workers are mostly men, many of whom send home remittances for family support, celebrations and fares, for investments and repayment of debts, and for retirement. Many remittances are actually taken home in the form of consumer goods, especially electrical appliances, radios and televisions. At any one time, workers abroad are many times more numerous than those at home, but they do not all send home remittances and individual families cannot rely on them; a 1980 survey found that 45% of rural households in Lesotho were headed by women and that fewer than half received any money from absent men (Haider, 1995: 85). No wonder that women learn to look after themselves, and that the gross enrolment rate of girls at primary and secondary levels in Lesotho exceeds that of boys, to a greater extent than in any other country in the world (Population Action International, 1998).

Much modern long-distance circulation of workers is extremely gender selective, and when the volume is great and the flows consistent it may have dramatic short-term impacts upon overall sex ratios at source and destination. An example of the effect at source is found in the Caribbean, where there has been a seasonal movement between the islands associated with the demand for mainly male labour on sugar cane, cotton and coffee plantations.

A much more numerically important example of the effect at destination is the current movement of millions of non-Arab Asian contract workers from the populous countries of Pakistan, India, Bangladesh, Sri Lanka and the Philippines to the relatively sparsely peopled but oil-rich Middle Eastern *Gulf States* of Bahrain, Kuwait, Oman, Qatar, Saudi Arabia and the United Arab Emirates (UAE). Although temporary contract workers, they have provided an essential labour force affecting the long-term sex ratios of those countries. In the smaller countries of Bahrain, Oman, Qatar and UAE, non-Arab workers from South and South-East Asia have long out-numbered those from the neighbouring Arab countries of the Middle East; as long ago as 1970 nearly two-thirds of non-nationals in Qatar were Iranians, Pakistanis and Indians. Arab workers were much more prepon-derant in Saudi Arabia and Kuwait prior to the Gulf War of 1991, but because many of them (e.g. Yemenis, Jordanians and Palestinians) sup-ported Iraq in that conflict they were seen to pose a possible political threat and so were expelled or had their contracts terminated. They were largely replaced by non-Arab Asians, mostly men contracted for work in the oil and construction industries and relatively few are found among the skilled expatriates, who generally come from Europe or other parts of the Middle East, but there are also considerable numbers of non-Arab Asian women who are usually from low-income families and forced by economic pressures to go overseas for work in domestic and other services. Among workers from Sri Lanka, for example, women more frequently than men tend to cite financial reasons for working overseas, along with a concern for the education of their children (Gunatilleke, 1991). Although they are short-term workers with no individual rights or possibility of staying on, non-nationals have become essential to the economies of the Gulf States and so have become a persistent and prominent element of their populations. In several countries (Kuwait, Qatar and UAE), they have formed a majority alien proletariat, despite the desire of Gulf States to effect a better balance of nationals and non-nationals. This is particularly true in Kuwait since the Iraqi invasion and subsequent Gulf War, although the intentions have met with little success so far (Al-Ramadhan, 1995).

In all the Gulf States with the exception of Kuwait the non-national populations in the mid-1990s exhibited massively unbalanced sex ratios, with more than twice as many men as women (Table 5.1), and even in Kuwait after the war the imbalance was striking. However, the concentration of non-nationals is most evident within the larger cities of the smaller countries (e.g. Doha, Dubai, Abu Dhabi) where most developmental activities take place. As the sex ratios of the national populations of all but one country (UAE) of the Gulf States were remarkably uniform in the mid-1990s at 102–103 and about the world average (Table 5.1), naturally the influx of non-nationals is the key reason for the unbalanced sex ratios of the total populations of these countries. Their effect is most striking in Qatar and UAE, where non-nationals accounted for about two-thirds and just over three-quarters respectively of the small total populations (a little more than half a million and less than two and a half million respectively), and where their high sex ratios exceeding 250 caused overall sex ratios approaching 200, i.e. twice as many males as females. In Oman, the sex ratio of the non-national population was even more unbalanced (379), but because it only accounted for a little more than a quarter of the total population of two and one-quarter millions it had much less impact upon the overall sex ratio of the country's population (140). Oman also exemplified the ever-changing effects of international movements of labour, because before 1970 and the beginning of its oil boom, it constituted an important source of male labour for other Gulf States which had already benefited from oil wealth, and like Yemen and Somalia an important source of seafarers especially in the Indian Ocean. So the advent of the oil industry during the 1970s meant that Oman experienced a considerable turnround, in-movements of workers rapidly replacing out-movements. Yemen has not been so lucky, as the summary expulsion and return of

Table 5.1 Populations and Sex Ratios of Gulf States, 1996

Country	Total Pop. 000s	S.R.	National Pop. 000s	Per cent	S.R.	Non-National Pop. 000s	Per cent	S.R.
Bahrain	567	134	355	62.7	103	211	37.3	215
Kuwait	2026	124	693	34.2	102	1334	65.8	138
Oman	2240	142	1623	72.5	103	617	27.5	379
Qatar	568	199	133	23.5	102	435	76.5	252
Saudi Arabia	19814	127	14323	72.3	102	5491	27.3	232
U.A.E.	2393	198	643	26.9	107	1750	73.1	255

Source of data: UNESCWA (1997) *Demographic and Related Socio-Economic Data Sheets for Countries of the Economic and Social Commission for Western Asia as Assessed in 1996*, No. 9.

hundreds of thousands of workers from Saudi Arabia as a result of Yemeni support for Iraq during the Gulf War has not been offset by any newly found oil riches.

The effect of the non-national populations in the Gulf States on different age groups is even more striking, because of course they are heavily concentrated in the working age groups, essentially those aged 20–64 and particularly those aged 25–49. In the case of the small state of Qatar, where non-nationals accounted for 76.5% of the total population in 1996, they accounted for 89.6% of the men aged 20–64 and 70.1% of the women in that age group, but as many as 93.1% of the men aged 40–44 and 79.5% of the women. Small wonder that many social problems arise with so many foreigners far from home. In Oman, where the population is larger but the proportion of non-nationals is lower, the preponderance of men among the non-nationals gave rise to very high sex ratios ranging from 615 to 747 within the various 5-year age groups between 40 and 59. Although they have less effect on the equivalent age-sex ratios of the total population, the unbalanced sex ratios of the non-nationals once again give rise to social problems.

Analysis of the non-nationals in the Gulf States by nationality reveals further diversity of unbalanced sex ratios, as some nationalities are preponderantly male and others female, depending on their economic roles within the different countries. Furthermore, changes in the economies of these countries mean that the nationalities of the foreign workforces are constantly changing. One certainty is that the smaller oil-rich Gulf States will continue to require foreign workers for the foreseeable future. But some of the more populous Gulf States in this conservative region, as for example Saudi Arabia, are beginning to balance the pros and cons of continued dependence on large inflows of foreign workers against allowing more of their increasingly educated female populations to join their workforces. Such moves will have great implications for societies and gender balances in the Gulf.

As the spectrum of socio-economic development in the world widens and the efficiency of international travel increases, there can be little doubt that long-distance circulation of both men and women will increase within the 'global village', that it will replace much long-distance migration but also that it will result in more definitive migration.

CHAPTER 6

THE FUTURE

Populations are never very predictable. Despite considerable improvements in the practice of population projections, erroneous predictions of future population totals have been commonplace, invariably because they have been excessively based on the continuation of recent and current linear trends. The further they look into the future, the more unreliable the projections (Lutz, Vaupel and Ahlburg, 1998). Inevitably, such projections have failed to consider the unforeseeable, the future occurrence of major physical and human catastrophes, shifts and discontinuities that change the course of human history and greatly affect population numbers, often making a nonsense of projections based on current trends (Clarke, 1997). Among the many examples of more or less abrupt shifts and events that changed the course of the twentieth century, greatly affecting local, national and/or international population dynamics, and consequently sex ratios, and yet were difficult to forsee, are the following:

- the two major world wars and a host of other international and internal conflicts, often arising from ethnic and religious divisions;
- the enormous movements of millions of displaced persons and refugees;
- the impact of vast pandemics like those of influenza and AIDS;
- the advent and rapid diffusion of antibiotics and much improved contraception, and their dramatic effects upon levels of mortality and fertility;
- the proliferation of new states in the second half of the century, with different levels of control over populations and of impact upon demographic transition;
- the rise and fall of communism;
- the globalisation of production and the emergence of newly industrialising countries;
- the huge growth and increasing complexity of the service sector, affecting all countries;

- the rapidly changing roles and status of women;
- the revolution in different means of transport and the impact on human mobility;
- the vast increase in international tourism;
- the advent and surge of mega-cities, especially in developing countries;
- the recent mercurial growth in electronic communications;
- the localised effects of innumerable natural disasters (e.g. floods, droughts, typhoons, hurricanes, earthquakes); and
- the growing human impacts on global environmental change.

Although an impressive list as it stands, it may be greatly extended by events that have had particular local significance upon populations, and it is certain that there will be many more unforeseen shifts, human and natural and of short and long duration, during the twenty-first century. With so many indirect influences upon human population numbers, it is naturally difficult to select those which are likely to have the major influence upon changing fertility, mortality and mobility, the three variables that affect directly the subtle differences in the relative numbers of males and females. But, as we have seen in our previous analyses of these three differentials, the prediction problem as far as sex ratios are concerned varies substantially according to the scale of the population considered. In small, local populations, gender differences in migration are the critical variable because the annual incidence of migration is usually greater than that of either births or deaths. In continental populations, on the other hand, sex-differentials in deaths and more recently in births play a more important role because long-term inter-continental migration is restricted and still of less numerical significance.

It is evident that many scientific advances and many social, economic and political processes are currently under way which may modify existing patterns of sex ratios from the immediate locality to the world population as a whole. Many will certainly affect the population dynamics of populations all over the world well before the target dates for the present rather speculative long-term population projections, such as those for 2050 and the even more tentative projections for 2150 (Lutz, 1994). We have pointed to the current impact of sex-selective abortions in the huge Asian populations of China and India, as well as the possible future effects of pre-implantation sex predetermination, especially if this technology is readily adopted within those and other populous countries where son preference persists. Surely improvements in contraceptive technology, still at a fairly rudimentary level, when allied with spiralling advances in genetic engineering will bring about a transformation in the reproductive choices available to couples. Not all of the world s major cultures will be equally receptive to such advances, and inevitably the rich will have more choice than the poor, but the present evidence of multinational fertility declines indicate that millions of couples world-wide are controlling their reproduction and would want to avail themselves of any increased reproductive choice. How will this affect the relative numbers of baby boys and girls? Much will depend on the differing rates of progress in the advancement of women within the various cultural realms. All the current evidence suggests that those cultural differences will persist well into the twenty-first century.

One of the few certainties about present population predictions is that the average age of almost all populations will rise, and that the quicker the decline in fertility the quicker the rise. Slower population growth means faster ageing of population. Moreover, everywhere there will be a major increase in the proportion of older people, to the extent that in parts of Asia and Latin America the population aged 60 and over is expected to double within the period 1990–2030. With very few exceptions, older populations mean a preponderance of older women, and at present there would appear to be no scientific advances in sight that would radically change that situation. The gap between male and female longevity is growing and likely to continue to do so, unless there is major progress in reducing the mortality of older men.

It is evident that a crucial influence upon sex ratios in the twenty-first century will be the variable rate of rise in the status of women, which affects all aspects of population dynamics. Rising status and changing gender roles have been nearly universal during the second half of the twentieth century, but there has been a steep gradient between on the one hand the high levels achieved in the most advanced countries such as the United States and Sweden, where rising status is having profound effects on commercial, social and political affairs as well as on lower fertility and mortality and more migration, and on the other hand the much more limited progress attained in the world's poorest countries in Sub-Saharan Africa, where cultural and economic constraints mean that too many women remain illiterate, uneducated, subordinated and often subjugated. Unfortunately, there are few signs that the spectrum is diminishing; quite the opposite. Continued progress is expected in most countries, but there should be major concerted efforts by all international organisations and national governments to reduce the current gender inequalities.

BIBLIOGRAPHY

Adams, J. (1999) *The Social Implications of Hypermobility*. The Environment Directorate, Organisation for Economic Cooperation and Development: Paris.

Adepoju, A. and Oppong, C. (1994) *Gender, Work and Population in Sub-Saharan Africa*. Published on behalf of the International Labour Office by James Currey: London and Heinemann: Portsmouth, New Hampshire.

Agnihotri, S.B. (1995) Missing females: a disaggregated analysis, *Economic and Political Weekly*, 30(33), 2074–84.

Al-Ramadhan, M.A. (1995) New population policy in Kuwait: the quest for a balance in the population composition, *Population Bulletin of ESCWA*, 43, 29–53.

Anderson, B.A. and Silver, B.D. (1995) Ethnic differences in fertility and sex ratios at birth in China: evidence from Xinjiang, *Population Studies*, 49(2), 211–26.

Anderson, D. (1997) *The Russian Mortality Crisis: Causes, Policy Responses, Lessons*. IUSSP Policy & Research Papers, 11.

Andersson, R. and Bergström, S. (1998) Is maternal malnutrition associated with a low sex ratio at birth? *Human Biology*, 70(6), 1101–6.

Arnold, F. (1985) Measuring the effect of sex preference on fertility: the case of Korea, *Demography*, 22(2), 280–88.

Arnold, F. (1986) The effect of sex preference on fertility and family planning: empirical evidence, *Population Bulletin of the United Nations*, No. 19.

Arnold, F. and Liu, Z. (1986) Sex preference, fertility and family planning in China, *Population and Development Review*, 12(2), 221–46.

Arnold, F., Choe, M.K. and Roy, T.K. (1996) *Son Preference, the Family-Building Process, and Child Mortality in India.* National Family Health Survey Subject Report. International Institute for Population Sciences and East-West Center Program on Population: Mumbai.

Astolfi, P. and Zonta, L.A. (1999) Sex ratio and parental age gap, *Human Biology*, 71(1), 135–41.

Atkins, P.J., Townsend, J.G., Raju, S. and Kumar, N. (1997) A geography of the sex ratio in India, *Espace, Populations, Sociétés*, 2/3, 161–71.

Avdeev, A., Blum, A., Zakharov, S. and Andreev, E. (1997) Réaction d'une population hétérogène à une perturbation. Un modèle d'interprétation des évolutions de mortalité en Russie, *Population*, 52(1), 7–44.

Bandarage, A. (1997) *Women, Population and Global Crisis. A Political-Economic Analysis.* Zed Books: London.

Battistella, G. and Paganoni, A. (1996) *Asian Women in Migration.* Scalabrini Migration Center: Quezon City, Philippines.

Bennholdt-Thompson, V. (1984) A theory of the sexual division of labour, in J. Smith, I. Wallerstein and H. Deiter-Evers eds. *Households and the World Economy.* Sage: Beverly Hills, 201–31.

Bilsborrow, R.E., Oberai, A.S. and Standing, G. (1984) *Migration Surveys in Low-Income Countries.* Croom Helm: Beckenham, Kent.

Bittles, A.H. *et al.* (1993) Sex ratio determinants in Indian populations: studies at national, state and district levels, in L.M. Schell, M.T. Smith and A. Bilsborough eds. *Urban Ecology in the Third World.* Cambridge University Press: Cambridge, 244–59.

Blake, G.H. (1999) *State Borders in a Globalising World.* Inaugural Lecture, University of Durham, December.

Bongaarts, J. and Bulatao, R.A. (1999) Completing the demographic transition, *Population and Development Review*, 25(3), 515–29.

Boserup, E. (1970) *Women's Role in Economic Development*. Allen & Unwin: London.

Boyle, P. and Halfacree, K. (1995) Service class migration in England and Wales 1980–1: identifying gender specific mobility patterns, *Regional Studies*, 29, 43–57.

Boyle, P., Halfacree, K. and Robinson, V. (1998) *Exploring Contemporary Migration*. Addison Wesley Longman: Harlow.

Boyle, P. and Halfacree, K. eds. (1999) *Migration and Gender in the Developed World*. Routledge: London and New York.

Brass, W., Coale, A.J., Demeny, P., Heisel, D.F., Lorimer, F., Romaniuk, A. and Van de Walle, E. (1968) *The Demography of Tropical Africa*. Princeton University Press: Princeton, New Jersey.

Brockerhoff, M. and Eu, H. (1993) Demographic and socioeconomic determinants of female rural to urban migration in Sub-Saharan Africa, *International Migration Review*, 27, 557–77.

Brydon, L. and Chant, S. (1989) *Women in the World. Gender Issues in Rural and Urban Areas*. Gower: Aldershot.

Campani, G. (1995) Women migrants: from marginal subjects to social actors, in R. Cohen ed., *The Cambridge Survey of World Migration*. Cambridge University Press: Cambridge, 546–50.

Caplan, P. (1985) *Class and Gender in India*. Tavistock: London.

Census Research Unit, Department of Geography, University of Durham (1980) *People in Britain. A Census Atlas*. HMSO: London.

Chahnazarian, A. (1988) Determinants of the sex ratio at birth: review of recent literature, *Social Biology*, 35, 214–35.

Chant, S. ed. (1992) *Gender and Migration in Developing Countries*. Belhaven: London.

Chen, M.A. ed. (1998) *Widows in India. Social Neglect and Public Action*. Sage: New Delhi.

Chesnais, J-C. (1999) L'homicide et le suicide dans le monde industriel. Le cas russe, *Population*, 54(1), 127–30.

Clarke, J.I. (1960) Rural and urban sex-ratios in England and Wales, *Tijdschrift voor Economische en Sociale Geografie*, 51(2), 21–38.

Clarke, J.I. ed. (1966) *Sierra Leone in Maps*. University of London Press: London.

Clarke, J.I. (1971) *Population Geography and the Developing Countries*. Pergamon Press: Oxford.

Clarke, J.I. (1973) Population in movement, in M. Chisholm and H.B. Rodgers eds., *Studies in Human Geography*. Heinemann Educational Books for SSRC: London.

Clarke, J.I. (1976) Population and scale: some general considerations, in L.A. Kosinski and J.W. Webb eds. *Population at Micro-Scale*. New Zealand Geographical Society and IGU Commission on Population Geography: Hamilton, New Zealand, 21–9.

Clarke, J.I. (1997) *The Future of Population*. Phoenix: London.

Clarke, J.I. and Fisher, W.B. eds. (1972) *Populations of the Middle East and North Africa*. University of London Press: London.

Clarke, J.I., Curson, P., Kayastha, S.L. and Nag, P. eds. (1989) *Population and Disaster*. Blackwell in association with the International Geographical Union Commission on Population Geography: Oxford.

Clarke, J.I. and Rhind, D.W. (1976) The relationship between the size of areal units and the characteristics of population structure, in L.A. Kosinski and J.W. Webb eds. *Population at Micro-Scale*. New Zealand Geographical Society and IGU Commission on Population Geography: Hamilton, New Zealand, 55–64.

Coale, A. (1991) Excess female mortality and the balance of the sexes in the population: an estimate of the number of missing females, *Population and Development Review*, 17(3), 517–23.

Coale, A. and Banister, J. (1994) Five decades of missing females in China, *Demography*, 31(3), 459–86.

Coleman, D. (1996) *Europe's Population in the 1990s*. Oxford University Press: Oxford.

Coney, N.S. and Mackey, W.C. (1996) Weinberg's Rule versus facultative sex ratio: an impasse in need of Occam's razor, *Mankind Quarterly*, 37(2), 187–201.

Courbage, Y. (1991) Surmortalité féminine chez les musulmans de Yougoslavie: Islam ou culture méditerranéenne? *Population*, 46(2), 299–325.

Craig, J. (1995) Males and females – some vital differences, *Population Trends*, 80, 26–30.

Curson, P. (1981) Remittances and migration – the commerce of movement, *Population Geography*, 3(1 and 2), 77–95.

Das Gupta, M. and Mari Bhat, P.N. (1997) Fertility decline and increased manifestation of sex bias in India, *Population Studies*, 51(3), 307–15.

Davis, D.L., Gottlieb, M.B. and Stampnitzky, J.R. (1998) Reduced ratio of male to female births in several industrial countries, *Journal of the American Medical Association*, 279(13), 1018–23.

De Oliveira, O. (1991) Migration of women, family organisation and labour markets in Mexico, in E. Jelin ed. *Family, Household and Gender Relations in Latin America*. Kegan Paul International: London, 101–18.

Decroly, J-M. and Vanlaer, J. (1991) *Atlas de la Population Européenne*. Editions de l'Université de Bruxelles: Brussels.

DeGraff, D.S. and Anker, R. (1999) *Gender, Labour Markets and Women's Work*. International Union for the Scientific Study of Population: Liège.

Devis, T.L.F. and Southworth, N.R. (1984) The study of internal migration in Great Britain, in A.J. Boyce ed., *Migration and Mobility. Biosocial Aspects of Human Movement*. Taylor & Francis: London & Philadelphia, 275–99.

Dewdney, J. and White, P. (1986) Portugal, in A. Findlay and P. White eds. *West European Population Change*. Croom Helm: London, 187–207.

Drèze, J. and Sen, A. (1995) *India: Economic Development and Social Opportunity*. Oxford University Press: Delhi.

Dyer, C. (1978) *Population and Society in Twentieth Century France*. Hodder and Stoughton: London.

Dyson, T. and Moore, M. (1983) Kinship structure, female autonomy, and demographic behavior in India, *Population and Development Review*, 9(1), 35–60.

Eshleman, J. Ross (2000) *The Family*. 9th ed., Allyn and Bacon: Boston.

Fairhurst, J., Booysen, I. and Hattingh, P. eds. (1997) *Migration and Gender. Place, Time and People Specific*. Department of Geography, University of Pretoria, South Africa, on behalf of the IGU Commission on Gender and Geography and the IGU Commission on Population Geography.

Fan, C. Cindy and Huang, Y. (1999) Female marriage migration in China, in G.P. Chapman, A.K. Dutt and R.W. Bradnock eds. *Urban Growth and Development in Asia*, vol. II *Living in Cities*. Ashgate: Aldershot, Brookfield, USA, 303–28.

Fauve-Chamoux, A. (1998) Le surplus urbain des femmes en France préindustrielle et le rle de la domesticité, *Population*, 53(1–2), 359–78.

Fawcett, J., Khoo, S-E. and Smith, P.C. eds. (1984) *Women in the Cities of Asia: Migration and Urban Adaptation*. Westview: Boulder, Colorado.

Findley, S.E. (1999) *Women on the Move. Perspectives on Gender Changes in Latin America*. International Union for the Scientific Study of Population: Liège.

Frederici, N., Mason, K.O. and Sogner, S. eds. (1993) *Women's Position and Demographic Change*. Clarendon Press: Oxford.

Gabaccia, D. (1996) Women of the mass migrations: from minority to majority, 1820–1930, in D. Hoerder and L.P. Moch eds. *European Migrants*. Northeastern University Press: Boston, 90–111.

Garvey, D. (1983) The history of migration flows in the Republic of Ireland, *Population Trends*, 39, 22–30.

Godfray, H.C.J. and Werren, J.H. (1996) Recent developments in sex ratio studies, *Trends in Ecology and Evolution*, 11(2), A59-A63.

Goodkind, D. (1996) On substituting sex preference strategies in East Asia: Does prenatal sex selection reduce postnatal discrimination?, *Population and Development Review*, 22(1), 111–25.

Goodkind, D. (1999) Should prenatal sex selection be restricted? Ethical questions and their implications for research and policy, *Population Studies*, 53(1), 49–61.

Gordon, I. (1995) Migration in a segmented labour market, *Transactions of the Institute of British Geographers*, 20(2), 139–55.

Grant, V.J. (1995) On sex ratio and coital rate: a hypothesis without foundation, *Current Anthropology*, 36(2), 295–8.

Green, A.E. (1994) The geography of changing female activity rates: issues and implications for policy and methodology, *Regional Studies*, 28, 633–9.

Green, A.E. (1995) The geography of dual career households: a research agenda and selected evidence from secondary data sources for Britain, *International Journal of Population Geography*, 1(1), 29–50.

Green, A.E., Hogarth, T. and Shackleton, R.E. (1999) Longer distance commuting as a substitute for migration in Britain: a review of trends, issues and implications, *International Journal of Population Geography*, 5(1), 49–67.

Gu, B. and Roy, K. (1995) Sex ratio at birth in China, with reference to other areas in East Asia: what we know, *Asia-Pacific Population Journal*, 10(3), 17–42.

Gugler, J. (1997) Gender and rural-urban migration: regional contrasts and the gender transition, in J. Fairhurst *et al.* eds. *op.cit.*, 83–100.

Gugler, J. and Ludwar-Ene, G. (1995) Gender and migration in Africa South of the Sahara, in J.Baker and T. Akin Aina eds. *The Migration Experience in Africa*. Nordiska Afrikainstitutet: Uppsala, 257–68.

Gunatilleke, G. ed. (1991) *Migration to the Arab World: Experience of Returning Migrants*. United Nations University Press: Tokyo.

Guttentag, M. and Secord, P.F. (1983) *Too Many Women? The Sex Ratio Question*. Sage: Beverly Hills.

Haider, R. (1996) *Gender and Development*. The American University in Cairo Press: Cairo.

Halfacree, K. (1995) Household migration and the structure of patriarchy: evidence from the USA, *Progress in Human Geography*, 19, 159–82.

Hall, R., Ogden, P.E. and Hill, C. (1997) The pattern and structure of one-person households in England and Wales and France, *International Journal of Population Geography*, 3(2), 161–81.

Hamilton, L. and Seyfrit, C. (1993) Town-village contrasts in Alaskan youth aspirations, *Arctic*, 46, 255–63.

Hampton, J. (1998) *Internally Displaced People. A Global Survey*. Earthscan: London.

Hart, N. (1989) Sex, gender and survival: inequalities of life chances between European men and women, in J. Fox ed. *Health Inequalities in European Countries*. Gower: Aldershot, 109–41.

Hausfater, G. and Hrdy, S.B. (1984) *Infanticide. Comparative and Evolutionary Perspectives*. Aldine de Gruyter: New York.

Hertrich, V. and Locoh, T. (1999) *Rapports de genre, formation et dissolution des unions dans les pays en développement*. International Union for the Scientific Study of Population: Liège.

Hill, C.M. and Ball, H.L. (1999) Parental manipulation of postnatal survival and well-being: are parental sex preferences adaptive? in T.M. Pollard and S.B. Hyatt eds. *Sex, Gender and Health*. Cambridge University Press: Cambridge, 18–36.

Hoerder, D. and Moch, L.P. eds. (1996) *European Migrants*. Northeastern University Press: Boston.

Hoy, C. (1999) Gender preference for children and its consequence for migration in China, *Geografiska Annaler*, 81B (1), 41–53.

Hugo, G. (1999) *Gender and Migrations in Asian Countries*. International Union for the Scientific Study of Population: Liège.

Hull, T. (1990) Recent trends in sex ratios at birth in China, *Population and Development Review*, 16(1), 63–83.

Human Rights Watch/Asia (1996) *Death by Default: a Policy of Fatal Neglect in China's State Orphanages*. Human Rights Watch: New York.

Huntington, S. (1996) *The Clash of Civilisations and the Remaking of the World Order*. Simon and Schuster: New York.

Jackson, J. and Moch, L.P. (1996) Migration and the social history of Modern Europe, in D. Hoerder and L.P. Moch eds. *op.cit.*, 52–69.

James, W.H. (1987a) The human sex ratio. Part 1: a review of the literature, *Human Biology*, 59(5), 721–52.

James, W.H. (1987b) The human sex ratio. Part 2: a hypothesis and a program of research, *Human Biology*, 59(6), 873–900.

James, W.H. (1995) What stabilises the sex ratio? *Annals of Human Genetics*, 59(2), 243–9.

James, W.H. (1997a) Sex ratio, coital rate, hormones and time of fertilization within the cycle, *Annals of Human Biology*, 24(5), 403–9.

James, W.H. (1997b) Weinberg's rule and facultative sex ratios, *Mankind Quarterly*, 37(4), 437–41.

James, W.H. (1997c) The validity of inferences of sex-selective infanticide, abortion and neglect from unusual reported sex ratios at birth, *European Journal of Population*, 13(2), 213–7.

Jejeebhoy, S.J. (1995) *Women's Education, Autonomy, and Reproductive Behaviour. Experience from Developing Countries*. Clarendon Press: Oxford.

Johansson, S. and Nygren, O. (1991) The missing girls of China: a new demographic account, *Population and Development Review*, 17(1), 35–51.

Johnson, K., Huang, B. and Wang, L. (1998) Infant abandonment and adoption in China, *Population and Development Review*, 24(3), 469–510.

Jones, H. and Pardthaisong, L. (1998) Demographic interactions and developmental implications in population systems undergoing rapid transformation: findings from Northern Thailand, *Paper presented at Conference on Models and Theory in Population Geography*, University of Dundee, August 26–28.

King, R., Connell, J. and White, P. eds. (1995) *Writing Across Worlds. Literature and Migration*. Routledge: London.

Kishor, S. (1995) Gender differentials in child mortality: a review of the evidence, in M. Das Gupta, L.C. Chen and T.N. Krishnan eds. *Women's Health in India. Risk and Vulnerability*. Oxford University Press: Delhi, 19–54.

Koser, K. and Lutz, H. (1998) *The New Migration in Europe. Social Constructions and Social Realities*. Macmillan: Basingstoke.

Kraly, E.P. (1997) International migration statistics: issues of refugee migration, asylum and gender, in J. Fairhurst *et al.*, eds. *op.cit.*, 207–28.

Kumar, N., Raju, S., Atkins, P.J. and Townsend, J.G. (1997) Where angels fear to tread? Mapping women and men in India, *Environment and Planning A*, 29, 2207–15.

Kumm, J. and Feldman, M.W. (1997) Gene-culture evolution and sex ratios: II sex-chromosomal distorters and cultural preferences for offspring sex, *Theoretical Population Biology*, 52(1), 1–15.

Langer, W.L. (1974) Infanticide: a historical survey, *Journal of Psychohistory*, 1, 353–65.

Larsen, U., Chung, W. and Das Gupta, M. (1998) Fertility and son preference in Korea, *Population Studies*, 52(3), 317–25.

Lawson, V. (1998) Hierachical households and gendered migration in Latin America: feminist extensions to migration theory, *Progress in Human Geography*, 22, 39–53.

Légaré, J., Myers, G.C. and Tabah, L. (1993) *Synthesis of National Monographs on Population Ageing*. CICRED: Paris.

Lerchl, A. (1998) Seasonality of sex ratio in Germany, *Human Reproduction*, 13(5), 1401–2.

Li, N., Tuljapurkar, S. and Feldman, M.W. (1995) High sex ratio at birth and its consequences, *Chinese Journal of Population Science*, 7(3), 213–21.

Lindsey, J.K. and Altham, P.M.E. (1998) Analysis of the human sex ratio by using overdispersion models, *Journal of the Royal Statistical Society, Series C: Applied Statistics*, 47(1), 149–57.

Lopez, A.D. and Ruzicka, L.T. eds. (1983) *Sex Differentials in Mortality*. Australian National University: Canberra.

Lutz, W. ed. (1994) *The Future Population of the World. What Can We Assume Today?* IIASA and Earthscan: London.

Lutz, W., Vaupel, J.W. and Ahlburg, D.A. eds. (1998) *Frontiers of Population Forecasting*. A Supplement to the *Population and Development Review*, 24.

Mackay, J. (1993) *The State of Health Atlas*. Simon and Schuster: New York.

Manning, J.T., Anderson, R.H. and Shutt, M. (1997) Parental age group skews child sex ratio, *Nature*, 389, Scientific correspondence, 344.

Marcoux, A. (1998) The feminization of poverty: claims, facts, and data needs, *Population and Development Review*, 24(1), 131–9.

Marleau, J. and Maheu, M. (1998) Un garçon ou une fille? Le choix des femmes et des hommes à l'égard d'un seul enfant, *Population*, 53(5), 1033–42.

Martin, J.F. (1994) Changing sex ratios : the history of Havasupai fertility and its implications for the human sex ratio variation, *Current Anthropology*, 35(3), 255–80.

Martin, J.F. (1995) Hormonal and behavioural determinants of the secondary sex ratio, *Social Biology*, 42(3–4), 226–46.

Mason, K.O. and Jensen, A-M. eds. (1995) *Gender and Family Change in Industrialized Countries*. Clarendon Press: Oxford.

Matsui, Y. (1999) *Women in the New Asia. From Pain to Power*. Zed Books: London.

Mayer, P. (1999) India's falling sex ratios, *Population and Development Review*, 25(2), 323–43.

Meslé, F. and Vallin, J. (1998) Evolutions et variations géographiques de la surmortalité masculine: du paradoxe français à la logique russe, *Population*, 53(6), 1079–1102.

Miller, B. (1981) *The Endangered Sex*. Cornell University Press: Ithaca, N.Y.

Momsen, J. and Townsend, J. eds. (1987) *Geography of Gender in the Third World*. Hutchinson: London.

Morokvasic, M. ed. (1984) Women in migration, *International Migration Review*, 18(4) (special issue).

Murthi, M., Guio, A-C. and Drèze, J. (1995) Mortality, fertility and gender bias in India: a district-level analysis, *Population and Development Review*, 21(4), 745–82.

Nadarajah, T. (1983) The transition from higher female to higher male mortality in Sri Lanka, *Population and Development Review*, 9(2), 317–25.

Neft, N. and Levine, A.D. (1997) *Where Women Stand. An International Report on the Status of Women in 140 Countries, 1997–1998*. Random House: New York.

Neville, R.J.Warwick (1979) Sex and age distribution, in R.J. Warwick Neville and C. James O'Neill eds. *The Population of New Zealand. Interdisciplinary Perspectives*. Longman Paul: Auckland, 150–84.

Noin, D. (1991) *Atlas de la population mondiale*. RECLUS -La Documentation Française: Paris.

Noin, D. and Chauviré, Y. (1987) *La population française*. Masson: Paris.

Ogden, P. and Winchester, H. (1986) France, in Findlay, A. and White, P. eds. *West European Population Change*. Croom Helm: London.

Oppong, C. ed. (1987) *Sex Roles, Population and Development in West Africa*. Heinemann: Portsmouth (N.H.) and James Currey: London.

Page, H. and Lestaeghe, R. (1981) *Child-Spacing in Tropical Africa: Traditions and Change*. Academic Press: New York and London.

Park, C.B. and Cho, N.H. (1995) Consequences of son preference in a low fertility society: imbalance of the sex ratio at birth in Korea, *Population and Development Review*, 21(1), 59–84.

Pearson, M. (1987) Old wives and young midwives? Women as caretakers of health: the case of Nepal, in J. Momsen and J. Townsend eds. *op.cit.*, 85–115.

Pedraza, S. (1991) Women and migration: the social consequences of gender, *American Review of Sociology*, 17, 303–25.

Pollard, T.M. and Hyatt, S.B. (1999) Sex, gender and health: integrating biological and social perspectives, in T.M. Pollard and S.B. Hyatt eds. *Sex, Gender and Health*. Cambridge University Press: Cambridge, 1–17.

Pong, S.L. (1994) Sex preference and fertility in Peninsular Malaysia, *Studies in Family Planning*, 25(3), 137–48.

Pooley, C.G. and Turnbull, J. (1998) *Migration and Mobility in Britain since the Eighteenth Century*. UCL Press: London.

Pooley, C.G. and Turnbull, J. (1999) The journey to work: a century of change, *Area*, 31(3), 281–92.

Population Action International (1998) *Educating Girls: Gender Gaps and Gains*. 1998 Report on Progress towards World Population Stabilisation, Washington D.C.

Poston, D.L., Gu, B., Liu, P.P. and McDaniel, T. (1997) Son preference and the sex ratio at birth in China: a provincial level analysis, *Social Biology*, 44(1–2), 55–76.

Potts, M. and Short, R. (1999) *Ever Since Adam and Eve. The Evolution of Human Sexuality*. Cambridge University Press: Cambridge.

Prakash, B.A. ed. (1999) *Kerala's Economic Development. Issues and Problems.* Sage: New Delhi.

Premi, M.K. (1994) Female infanticide and child neglect as possible reasons for low sex ratios in the Punjab 1881–1931, *Population Geography*, 16(1–2), 33–48.

Raju, S., Atkins, P.J., Kumar, N. and Townsend, J.G. (1997) *Atlas of Women and Men in India.* Kali for Women: Delhi.

Raleigh, V.S. and Kiri, V.A. (1997) Life expectancy in England: variations and trends by gender, health authority and level of deprivation, *Journal of Epidemiology and Community Health*, 51(6), 649–58.

Ravenstein, E.G. (1885) The laws of migration, *Journal of the Royal Statistical Society*, 48, 167–227.

Reader, J. (1997) *Africa. A Biography of the Continent.* Hamish Hamilton: London.

Retherford, R.D. (1975) *The Changing Sex Differential in Mortality.* Greenwood: Westport, Connecticutt & London.

Riley, N. and Gardner, R.W. (1997) *China's Population: A Review of the Literature.* IUSSP: Liège.

Ross, J.A. ed. (1982) *International Encyclopaedia of Population.* 2 vols., Free Press: New York & London.

Rousham, E.K. (1999) Gender bias in South Asia: effects on child growth and nutritional status, in T.M. Pollard and S.B. Hyatt eds. *Sex, Gender and Health.* Cambridge University Press: Cambridge, 37–52.

Rowland, D.T. (1979) *Internal Migration in Australia.* Australian Bureau of Statistics: Canberra.

Rukannudin, A.R. and Farooqui, M.N.I. (1988) *The State of Population in Pakistan, 1987.* National Institute of Population Studies: Islamabad.

Seager, J. (1997) *The State of Women in the World Atlas.* New Edition, Penguin Reference: London.

Seidl, C. (1995) The desire for a son is the father of many daughters: a sex ratio paradox, *Journal of Population Economics*, 8(2), 185–203.

Shryock, H.S., Siegel, J.S. and Associates (1973) *The Methods and Materials of Demography*. 2nd, printing rev., U.S. Department of Commerce: Washington, D.C.

Sieff, D.F. (1990) Explaining biased sex ratios in human populations: a critique of recent studies, *Current Anthropology*, 31(1), 25–35.

Singelmann, J. (1993) Levels and trends of female internal migration in developing countries, 1960-1980, in *Internal Migration of Women in Developing Countries: Proceedings of the United Nations Expert Meeting on the Feminization of Internal Migration*. Aguascalientes, Mexico, 22–25 October 1991, United Nations: New York, 77–93.

Singh, J.S. (1998) *Creating a New Consensus on Population*. Earthscan: London.

Skeldon, R. (1990) *Population Mobility in Developing Countries*. Belhaven Press: London & New York.

Smith, A. (1997) *Sex, Genes and all That*. Macmillan: London.

South, S.J. (1988) Sex ratios, economic power, and women's roles: a theoretical extension and empirical test, *Journal of Marriage and the Family*, 50, 19–31.

South, S.J. and Trent, K. (1988) Sex ratios and women's roles: a cross national analysis, *American Journal of Sociology*, 93(5), 1096–1115.

Strickland, S.S. and Tuffrey, V.R. (1997) Parental investment theory and birth sex ratios in Nepal, *Journal of Biosocial Science*, 29(3), 283–95.

Suh, Moon-Hee (1995) Area differentials in sex imbalance in births, *Health and Social Welfare Review* (Korea), 15(2), 143–73.

Swindell, K. (1970) The distribution of age and sex characteristics in Sierra Leone and their relevance to a study of internal migration, *Tijdschrift voor Economische en Sociale Geografie*, 61(6), 366–73.

Teitelbaum, M. (1972) Factors associated with the sex ratio in human populations, in G.A. Harrison and A.J. Boyce eds. *The Structure of Human Populations*. Clarendon Press: Oxford, 90–109.

Thadani, V.N. and Todaro, M.P. (1979) Female migration in developing countries: a framework for analysis, *Center for Policy Working Paper* 47, Population Council: New York.

Thatcher, A.R. (1992) Trends in numbers and mortality at high ages in England and Wales, *Population Studies*, 46(3), 411–26.

Thierry, X (1999) Risques de mortalité et de surmortalité au cours de dix premières années de veuvage, *Population*, 54(2), 177–204.

Thompson, W.S. and Lewis, D.T. (1965) *Population Problems*. Fifth ed. McGraw-Hill: New York.

Trent, K. and South, S.J (1989) Structural determinants of the divorce rate: a cross-societal analysis, *Journal of Marriage and the Family*, 51, 391–404.

Tully. M. (1991) *No Full Stops in India*. Viking: London.

Ulizzi, L. and Zonta, L.A. (1994) Sex ratios and selection by early mortality in humans: fifty-year analysis in different ethnic groups, *Human Biology*, 66(6), 1037–48.

UNFPA (1997) *India: Towards Population and Development Goals*. Oxford University Press: Delhi.

UNFPA (1998) *The State of World Population 1998. The New Generations.* UNFPA: New York.

United Nations (1955) *Methods of Estimating Basic Demographic Measures from Incomplete Data*. Department of Economic and Social Affairs, Population Studies No. 23, Manual No. II.

United Nations (1982) *Population of India*. UN Economic and Social Commission for Asia and the Pacific, Country Monograph Series No. 10: New York.

United Nations (1990) *Global Outlook 2000. An Economic, Social and Environmental Perspective*. United Nations: New York.

United Nations (1991) *The World's Women 1970–1990: Trends and Statistics*. United Nations: New York.

United Nations (1993) *Demographic Yearbook. Special Issue: Population Aging and the Situation of Elderly Persons*. United Nations: New York.

United Nations (1996) *World Population Prospects: the 1996 Revision*. Department for Economic and Social Information and Policy Analysis: New York.

United Nations (1998) *World Urbanization Prospects: The 1996 Revision*. United Nations: New York.

United Nations (1999) *Demographic Yearbook, 1997*. United Nations: New York.

U.S. Bureau of Census, (1992) *An Aging World II*. US Department of Commerce, International Population Reports P95/92–3, 30–5.

Vallin, J. (1999) *Mortalitè, sexe et genre*. International Union for the Scientific Study of Population: Liège.

Warnes, A. (1999) Differential migrations through later life, in P. Boyle and K. Halfacree eds. *Migration and Gender in the Developed World*. Routledge: London, 294–309.

White, P. and Jackson, P. (1995) (Re)theorising population geography, *International Journal of Population Geography*, 1(2), 111–23.

Willis, K. ed. (2000) *Gender and Migration*. Edward Elgar: Cheltenham.

Wilmoth, J.R. (1998) Is the pace of Japanese mortality decline converging toward international trends? *Population and Development Review*, 24(3), 593–600.

Winston, R. (1997) *The Future of Genetic Manipulation*. Phoenix: London.

Wood, C. (1981) Structural changes and household strategies: a conceptual framework for the study of rural migration, *Human Organization*, 40(4), 338–44.

World Bank (1998) *World Development Indicators*. The World Bank: New York.

Zeng, Y., Tu, P., Gu, B., Xu, L., Li, B. and Li, Y. (1993) Causes and implications of the recent increase in the reported sex ratio at birth in China, *Population and Development Review*, 19(2), 283–302.

SUBJECT INDEX